PRACTICE MAKES PERFECT

A WORKBOOK OF GENEALOGICAL EXERCISES

*Compiled by the members of the Education Sub-Committee
of the Federation of Family History Societies*

Federation of Family History Societies

Published by the
Federation of Family History Societies
c/o The Benson Room, Birmingham and Midland Institute,
Margaret Street, Birmingham B3 3BS, England

Copyright © The Federation of Family History Societies 1993

ISBN 1 872094 64 3

Printed in Great Britain at the Alden Press, Oxford.

TABLE OF CONTENTS

ACKNOWLEDGEMENTS

The Federation of Family History Societies Education Sub-Committee members who have compiled this book are Libby Batchelor, Marcia Evans, Janet Few, Hilary Marshall, Geoff Swinfield, John Titford and Jill Valentine. Special thanks go to Libby Batchelor for all the typing and drawing up of family trees. Thanks are also due to those who have assisted in any way with this production.

The compilers are grateful to the following who have allowed the use of information and examples in the compilation of this book:-

Stuart Valentine for all the documents used in the Beecroft pedigree exercise.

Cornwall Record Office for permission to reproduce the will of William Ough and John Muffet.

Hereford and Worcester Record Office for permission to reproduce the will of Robert Baylis (reference BA 3585 008.7).

The Public Record Office for permission to reproduce information taken from census returns.

The General Register Office for permission to reproduce birth, marriage and death certificates.

The Principal Probate Registry for permission to reproduce material from their records.

The Institute of Heraldic and Genealogical Studies for examination questions and pedigrees.

FOREWORD

In 1989 the Institute of Heraldic and Genealogical Studies produced a new detailed Syllabus of Study listing the knowledge that a student should acquire at four different levels. Assessment tests are available at each of four levels based on a different proportion of the Syllabus. Using these tests a teacher may assess how much each student learned during a course. Students who have reached the appropriate level are issued with a certificate of attainment.

Examples, mainly taken from the level 'B' assessment tests of the Institute of Heraldic and Genealogical Studies, are included in this book. In the original tests, each paper consists of ten multiple choice questions, each with three possible answers, testing knowledge of a basic source, date or repository. These are followed by five questions which require a short answer of a phrase or one or two sentences. The third section requires the student to compile a small pedigree from a body of data for a given family and to suggest searches which could be used to extend the family tree of that line beyond the scope of the documentation provided.

It was believed that the publication of example test papers and the appropriate answers would be a useful teaching aid for all those who offer courses in the subject of genealogy and family history. Such papers could be used during a course for revision and once students realise their potential they should be more inclined to submit themselves for assessment at the end of the course. This booklet can also be used by individuals for further study and enjoyment.

Teachers who wish to enrol their students for assessments at level 'B' or any other level should obtain enrolment forms from the Institute of Heraldic and Genealogical Studies.

Assessment papers produced by the Institute are sent to the tutor whose students have enrolled. The completed scripts are returned to the Institute for marking, assessment and issue of certificates to successful candidates. A short written report is produced outlining the strengths and weaknesses of each student.

It is not a prerequisite of enrolment that a student should have attended a course run by the Institute of Heraldic and Genealogical Studies. However the student who wishes to test his or her knowledge should be familiar with the content of the Institute's Syllabus of Study available from the Registrar. The Syllabus describes the topics included in each level of assessment and further examinations leading to higher qualifications. Information can also be obtained about the twenty-four lecture accredited Correspondence Course.

Teachers who wish to use the tests with their students at the end of a course should also obtain a copy of the Syllabus of Study to ensure that they have included all necessary topics in their course of instruction. To help in this, the Institute has produced a series of Teachers' Packs. These are acetate overhead projection slides, each pack illustrating a topic from the Syllabus. A list of titles and prices is available from the Registrar of the Institute of Heraldic and Genealogical Studies, 79-82 Northgate, Canterbury, Kent, CT1 1BA.

INTRODUCTION

The number of classes in genealogy has increased dramatically over the past ten years. Those who teach the subject try to pass on to students a knowledge of sources, research method and technique. During the course students should become familiar with the documentation used in producing a genealogy and at the end should be able, if they wish, to test their acquired knowledge. Individuals can use these exercises for enjoyment or to assess their own progress.

For the purposes of this booklet and for the convenience of the teacher, examples have been divided into three sections; a fourth section contains the answers.

The first section of the booklet contains seventy multiple-choice questions divided into groups of ten. Each set deals with a different topic.

A	Societies, Libraries and Printed Sources
B	General Registration (England and Wales)
C	Census Returns (England and Wales)
D	Parish Registers and Bishop's Transcripts
E	Probate
F	Nonconformists and Their Records
G	Parish Chest and Finding Aids

The second section contains questions requiring students to fill in information rather than to pick an answer from a group of possibilities.

The third section consists of longer questions requiring the student to construct a pedigree from data relating to one family and then to suggest sources for further research.

The answers are to be found in the fourth section. These can be used by students if they are using the tests for revision purposes. Alternatively they can be used by the teacher to correct scripts if the questions are used during a course to test the achievement of the students. Fully documented pedigrees are the ideal in genealogical research but constraints of space in this booklet has meant that full details of individuals have not always been included. Suggestions for further research with the location of the source or the method by which this information could be ascertained are also given. Where possible indexes are used as finding aids to reduce the number of original documents which would need to be examined.

This booklet has been published through the Federation of Family History Societies to allow it to be distributed widely through family history societies to their members.

LIST OF ABBREVIATIONS USED IN THIS BOOK

ac	acre
ag lab	agricultural labourer
b.	born/birth
bach	bachelor
bpt	baptised
botp	both of this parish
bur	buried
c.	circa
d.	died
d.o.	daughter of
DSS	Department of Social Security
FFHS	Federation of Family History Societies
gent	gentleman
GRO	General Register Office
IGI	International Genealogical Index
IHGS	Institute of Heraldic and Genealogical Studies
Indep.	Independent
LDS	Church of Jesus Christ of Latter-Day Saints
lic	licence
m.	married
miw	mention in will of
Ms	Mistress
ofa	of full age
otp	of this parish
PCC	Prerogative Court of Canterbury
pr	probate; proved
PRO	Public Record Office
PPR	Principal Probate Registry
s.o.	son of
SOG	Society of Genealogists
sp	spinster
wid	widow
widr	widower
wit	witnesses

SECTION 1. SETS OF QUESTIONS WITH MULTIPLE CHOICE ANSWERS

This section contains seven sets of questions and each question has three possible answers. Tick the answer (a, b, or c) which you think is correct.

SET A. SOCIETIES, LIBRARIES AND PRINTED SOURCES.

1. What is the Journal of the Society of Genealogists called?
    (a) The Genealogist
    (b) The Genealogists' Magazine
    (c) Family History News and Digest

2. Which source book indexes most of the published genealogical material on family histories from 1903 to 1953?
    (a) Barrow : The Genealogist's Guide
    (b) Marshall : The Genealogist's Guide
    (c) Whitmore : A Genealogical Guide

3. What is the name of the magazine, published monthly, which gave notices of births, marriages and deaths between 1731 and 1861?
    (a) Notes and Queries
    (b) Annual Register
    (c) Gentleman's Magazine

4. Which of the following can be used to find individuals researching particular family names?
    (a) Genealogical Research Directory
    (b) Burke's Peerage and Baronetage
    (c) Genealogical Helper

5. What is the title of the journal of the Federation of Family History Societies?
    (a) Family History News and Digest
    (b) Family Tree Magazine
    (c) The Genealogists' Magazine

6. Which body can supply details of the whereabouts of the graves of British and other servicemen who died in the two World Wars?
    (a) Imperial War Museum
    (b) Commonwealth War Graves Commission
    (c) Ministry of Defence

7. Where is the National Newspaper Library?
    (a) Colindale
    (b) Somerset House
    (c) Society of Genealogists

8. Which society is now primarily concerned with publishing calendars and indexes to probate material?
    (a) Harleian Society
    (b) Royal Historical Society
    (c) British Record Society

9. Which organisation is open to those who are interested in all references to a particular surname?
    (a) British Genealogical Record Users Committee
    (b) Record Users Group
    (c) Guild of One Name Studies

10. Where might you find a 'D' manuscript?
    (a) IHGS
    (b) Society of Genealogists
    (c) William Salt Library

SET B. General Registration (England and Wales)

1. Where would you find the indexes of civil registration for England and Wales?
    - (a) St Catherine's House
    - (b) Somerset House
    - (c) Public Record Office

2. In which year was general registration introduced in England and Wales?
    - (a) 1827
    - (b) 1832
    - (c) 1837

3. From which year do the GRO indexes of deaths for England and Wales give the age of the deceased?
    - (a) 1911
    - (b) 1837
    - (c) 1866

4. From which year do the indexes of birth give the child's mother's maiden name?
    - (a) 1905
    - (b) 1911
    - (c) 1927

5. From which year were nonconformists allowed to marry in their own chapel without the presence of a local registration officer?
    - (a) 1837
    - (b) 1874
    - (c) 1898

6. From which year do the GRO indexes of marriage provide the surname of the other spouse?
    - (a) 1837
    - (b) 1895
    - (c) 1912

7. What was the legal age for marriage of girls with parental consent before 1929?
    - (a) 12
    - (b) 14
    - (c) 16

8. In which year do the reference numbers identifying registration districts change from Roman to Arabic numerals?
    - (a) 1852
    - (b) 1865
    - (c) 1946

9. In which year were strict legal penalties introduced against non-registration of births, marriages and deaths?
    - (a) 1837
    - (b) 1865
    - (c) 1874

10. From which year are records of adoption indexed at the General Register Office for England and Wales?
    - (a) 1851
    - (b) 1927
    - (c) 1911

SET C. CENSUS RETURNS (ENGLAND AND WALES)

1. Where is the Public Record Office census search room?
   - (a) Land Registry Building, Portugal Street
   - (b) Chancery Lane
   - (c) Kew

2. How should the age of a 68 year old man be recorded in the 1841 census returns?
   - (a) 65
   - (b) 68
   - (c) 70

3. Which is the last census available for public inspection in England and Wales?
   - (a) 1881
   - (b) 1891
   - (c) 1901

4. Which was the first census to ask for a person's place of birth?
   - (a) 1851
   - (b) 1861
   - (c) 1871

5. What is the call number of the 1851 census returns?
   - (a) RG 9
   - (b) BT 112
   - (c) HO 107

6. On which date was the 1861 census taken?
   - (a) 8 April
   - (b) 7 August
   - (c) 23 November

7. From which year did census returns become records of the Registrar General rather than the Home Office?
   - (a) 1851
   - (b) 1861
   - (c) 1871

8. Which census includes a question concerning the number of rooms inhabited by each household?
   - (a) 1891
   - (b) 1851
   - (c) 1841

9. Which census is the subject of a national indexing programme?
   - (a) 1861
   - (b) 1891
   - (c) 1881

10. From which year were abbreviations to indicate occupations not permitted in census returns?
   - (a) 1851
   - (b) 1891
   - (c) 1871

SET D. PARISH REGISTERS AND BISHOP'S TRANSCRIPTS

1. From which year were parish registers required to be copied out on to parchment?
    - (a) 1558
    - (b) 1812
    - (c) 1753

2. On which day did the church year begin in the 17th century?
    - (a) 1 January
    - (b) 25 March
    - (c) 6 April

3. When were Bishop's Transcripts generally introduced?
    - (a) 1538
    - (b) 1558
    - (c) 1597

4. In which year was the Gregorian Calendar first used in England?
    - (a) 1752
    - (b) 1607
    - (c) 1733

5. When were printed marriage registers introduced?
    - (a) 1733
    - (b) 1754
    - (c) 1775

6. In which year were separate baptismal and burial registers introduced in England and Wales?
    - (a) 1837
    - (b) 1753
    - (c) 1812

7. Acts of Parliament in 1667 and 1678 required that burials take place in a shroud made of what material?
    - (a) cotton
    - (b) linen
    - (c) wool

8. Which two religious bodies were exempt from Hardwicke's Marriage Act?
    - (a) Catholics and Jews
    - (b) Jews and Quakers
    - (c) Methodists and Catholics

9. When was it ordered that parish registers should be written in English?
    - (a) 1538
    - (b) 1649
    - (c) 1732

10. What is the meaning of the latin word UXOR in parish registers?
    - (a) wife
    - (b) farmer
    - (c) widower

SET E. PROBATE

1. When did the civil system of proving wills begin?
    (a) 1538
    (b) 1874
    (c) 1858

2. Where is the Principal Probate Registry for England and Wales?
    (a) St Catherine's House
    (b) Somerset House
    (c) Public Record Office

3. Where would you find the registered wills of the Prerogative Court of Canterbury?
    (a) Canterbury Cathedral Archives
    (b) Principal Probate Registry
    (c) Public Record Office, Chancery Lane

4. Where would a will normally be proved if the testator had property in one parish only?
    (a) Archdeacon's Court
    (b) Consistory or Commissary Court
    (c) Archbishop's Court

5. When was the Married Women's Property Act passed?
    (a) 1858
    (b) 1882
    (c) 1901

6. How old did a male have to be to make a will before 1837?
    (a) 10
    (b) 12
    (c) 14

7. In 1837 what was decreed to be the minimum age at which either a man or a woman could make a will?
    (a) 18
    (b) 21
    (c) 25

8. From which year was a tax levied on wills and administrations?
    (a) 1775
    (b) 1796
    (c) 1817

9. At which record repository would you expect to find wills proved by the Prerogative Court of York?
    (a) Borthwick Institute
    (b) Department of Palaeography and Diplomatic, Durham University
    (c) Lichfield Diocesan Record Office

10. Where could you examine Welsh wills, with the exception of those proved in the PCC, proved before the beginning of the civil system.
    (a) National Library of Wales, Aberystwyth
    (b) University of Wales College, Cardiff
    (c) Dyfed Archives Office, Aberystwyth

SET F. NONCONFORMISTS AND THEIR RECORDS

1. Which London prison was the venue for many 'clandestine marriages' between 1660 and 1753?
    - (a) Bridewell
    - (b) The Fleet
    - (c) Newgate

2. What type of document records the oaths sworn in 1641/2 in defiance of popery?
    - (a) Hardwicke's Marriage Act
    - (b) Compton's Census
    - (c) Protestation Returns

3. Where are the majority of Quaker records kept?
    - (a) Public Record Office, Kew
    - (b) Dr Williams's Library
    - (c) Friends House

4. Where are the nonconformist registers collected between 1837 and 1840 to be found?
    - (a) St Catherine's House
    - (b) Public Record Office, Chancery Lane
    - (c) Public Record Office, Kew

5. Which library registered nonconformist births between 1742 and 1837?
    - (a) Dr Williams's Library
    - (b) Fawcett Library
    - (c) Society of Friends Library

6. Where would you find the largest collection of biographical material for Methodists?
    - (a) Public Record Office, Chancery Lane
    - (b) John Rylands Library, Manchester
    - (c) Society of Genealogists

7. Recusant Rolls record the fines primarily imposed on which religious sect?
    - (a) Quakers
    - (b) Jews
    - (c) Catholics

8. Who allowed Jews to return to live in England?
    - (a) Henry VIII
    - (b) Oliver Cromwell
    - (c) Queen Victoria

9. In which year was the ecclesiastical census organised by Compton?
    - (a) 1642
    - (b) 1662
    - (c) 1676

10. Which religious sect normally lists in their records many of those present at a marriage ceremony?
    - (a) Quakers
    - (b) Countess of Huntingdon's Connection
    - (c) Moravians

SET G. PARISH CHEST AND FINDING AIDS

1. In which year was the Poor Relief Act passed which introduced important poor law documentation concerning right of settlement?
    (a) 1558
    (b) 1812
    (c) 1662

2. What document identifies a person's rights to receive poor relief if necessary?
    (a) Removal Order
    (b) Settlement Certificate
    (c) Churchwarden's Accounts

3. In which year were Union Workhouses introduced?
    (a) 1813
    (b) 1834
    (c) 1837

4. Which finding aid lists marriages and baptisms by county?
    (a) Boyd
    (b) Pallot
    (c) IGI

5. Where would you find the original copy of Boyd's Marriage Index?
    (a) Guildhall Library
    (b) British Library
    (c) Society of Genealogists

6. Which marriage index mainly contains events which took place in the London area between 1780 and 1837?
    (a) Pallot's Marriage Index
    (b) Boyd's Marriage Index
    (c) Selon Index

7. Which of these documents might you expect to find with the parish chest material?
    (a) will
    (b) tithe map
    (c) bishop's transcript

8. In which year were parish chests introduced for the protection of parochial documentation?
    (a) 1538
    (b) 1662
    (c) 1753

9. What was a glebe terrier?
    (a) a survey of a clergyman's benefice
    (b) a parish dog
    (c) a local beggar and troublemaker

10. In which year were tithe dues commuted from kind to monetary payments resulting in the production of tithe maps?
    (a) 1662
    (b) 1796
    (c) 1836

SECTION 2. QUESTIONS REQUIRING SHORT ANSWERS

Each question in this section requires a phrase or one or two sentences as an answer.

SET A

1. How would Helen Jones, who had the maiden name Higgins and who had previously been married to a Mr. Wilson, be recorded on the birth certificate of her child by Mr. Jones?

2. Give two pieces of personal information which are not shown in the 1841 census but which appear in the 1851 census.

3. List the personal information that you should find on the full English or Welsh birth certificate of a legitimate child before 1969.

4. What do the following abbreviations stand for in the Census Returns?
   (a) unm.   (b) J.   (c) ag. lab.   (d) F.S.   (e) F.W.K.

5. What is wrong with a death certificate on which the date of registration is given as 10 Aug 1887 and the date of death as 31 July 1887?

SET B

1. Who is:
   (a) an executrix   (b) a testatrix   (c) a relict?

2. What does 'half baptised' mean? What entry might you find in a parish register with, or shortly after, such an entry?

3. What name was given in most areas to the copies made of parish register entries of baptism, marriage and burial? How often were these made and to whom were they sent?

4. What information would you discover from the parish register entry for a marriage between 1754 and 1837?

5. Give the English version of the following Latin names: Andreas, Guilielmus, Johanna, Jacobus, Villefridus and the full version of the following abbreviated names: Xpr, Jas, Wm, Thos, Jno.

SET C

1. What do the following abbreviations stand for, in association with wills?
   (a) PPR   (b) cod   (c) admon   (d) inv   (e) exec   (f) PCC

2. List four classes of people who were barred from making wills by the 1540 Statute of Wills.

3. What information should you be able to obtain from the indexes to post-1858 probate records at Somerset House?

4. In which courts are the wills of people with property in these places most likely to have been proved?
   (a) Lancashire and Yorkshire   (b) Lancashire and Essex   (c) Essex and Hampshire

5. What is a probate inventory?

SET D

1. What would you find in the 'Great Book of Sufferings'?

2. What do the following abbreviations stand for?
        (a) b.o.t.p.   (b) d.s.p.   (c) unm.   (d) ob.

3. Describe two ways in which you might locate a missing living relative.

4. List four sources from which you could discover if anyone was already researching your family.

5. What do the following abbreviations stand for:
        (a) NGD   (b) GRD   (c) LDS   (d) GOONS   (e) FFHS   (f) SOG   (g) IHGS

SET E

1. What do the letters O.P.C.S. stand for?

2. What document would you be seeking if you wrote to Smedley Hydro?

3. What does a time of day in the 'when and where born' column of an English or Welsh birth certificate usually indicate?

4. What is the difference between an abstract and a transcript?

5. Names three indexes that you might check if you were looking for a marriage which took place in 1805.

SET F

1. Give three ways by which a person could claim a parish as his or her legal place of settlement according to the Poor Law statutes of the 18th century.

2. Which three types of document resulted when a couple applied for permission to marry by licence before 1837?

3. Give a brief explanation of the differences between the Trade, Commercial and Court sections of a directory.

4. A family is recorded in the 1851 census as follows:

Burke Street	John Molineaux	Head	mar.	47	Agricultural Labr.	Ireland
	Maria	"	wife	mar.	49		France
	Philip	"	son	unm.	27	Agricultural Labr.	London
	Sarah	"	dau	unm.	22	" "	Kent, Snodland
	William	"	son		8	Scholar	" "

How would you expect the same family to appear ten years earlier in the 1841 returns of Snodland, Kent?

5. Name three documents, found amongst family muniments, which provide an age for an individual in association with a date.

SECTION 3. DATA PACKS FOR COMPILING PEDIGREE EXERCISES

In this section you are required to compile a pedigree (family tree) from the data provided for each family. There are ten examples. You should then suggest searches which could be conducted to confirm the family tree that you have completed and also to extend that line beyond the scope of the documentation provided to an earlier period. The location of the suggested record or index should be specified. If this is not known the title of the source book which you would examine to allow its location to be determined should be included in the answer.

A. BEECROFT OF BLEASBY, NOTTINGHAMSHIRE

Document A: National Health Insurance Acts 1911 Certificate.

This Form must NOT be sent to the Registrar-General.

(This Form of Requisition is furnished gratuitously. The Applicant must fill in the required particulars, sign his or her name at the foot, and either take the form to the Superintendent Registrar of the District in which the Birth occurred, or send it to him, together with the fee of 6d. and a stamped and addressed envelope.)

NATIONAL HEALTH INSURANCE ACTS, 1911 TO 1920, AND UNEMPLOYMENT INSURANCE ACT, 1920.

ENGLAND AND WALES.

Requisition for a Certificate of Birth prescribed under Section 114 of the National Insurance Act, 1911, and Section 32 of the Unemployment Insurance Act, 1920.

To the SUPERINTENDENT REGISTRAR or other person having the custody of the Register Book in which the Birth of the under-mentioned person is recorded.

I, the undersigned, hereby demand for the purposes of the

(a) National Health Insurance Acts, 1911 to 1920,

or

(b) Unemployment Insurance Act, 1920,

(If the application is made for purposes of Health Insurance, strike out paragraph (b) ; if for purposes of Unemployment Insurance, strike out paragraph (a).)

a Certificate of the Birth of the person in relation to whom particulars are given below.

Name of Person in full.....*Nicholas William Beecroft*

Date of Birth—The *10* day of *Febuary*......One thousand *eight*

hundred and *sixty five* (The year to be written in words, not figures.)

Place of Birth.....*Bleasby*

Father's Name (in full).....*Edwin Beecroft*

Father's Occupation.....*Labourer*

Mother's Name (in full).....*Jane Beecroft*

Mother's Maiden Surname.....*Simon*

Approved Society, Association, Insurance Committee, Employment Exchange, or other Body or Person for whom the Certificate is required.....*Employment Exchange Derby*

Signature of Applicant.....*N W Beecroft*

Address.....*161 Watson Street Derby*

Dated this *3* day of *November* 192*4*

The above Form of Requisition was prescribed by the Minister of Health by Order No. 1932, dated 26th October, 1920.

A. BEECROFT OF BLEASBY, NOTTINGHAMSHIRE (continued)

Document B. Death Certificate Nicholas William Beecroft.

Dp 061691

The Statutory Fee for this Certificate is 2s. 7d.
If required subsequently to registration, a
Search Fee is payable in addition.

[Printed by authority of the Reg

CERTIFIED COPY of an ENTRY OF DEATH.

Pursuant to the Births and Deaths Registration Acts, 1836 to 1929.

Registration District Derby

Death in the Sub-district of Derby North West in the County Borough of Derby

No.	When and where Died.	Name and Surname.	Sex.	Age.	Rank or Profession.	Cause of Death.	Signature, Description, and Residence of Informant.	When Registered.	Signature of Registrar.
Columns:— 1		2	3	4	5	6	7	8	9
424	Tenth July 1934 Derby City Hospital R.D.	Nicholas William Beecroft	Male	63	of 161. Watson Street Derby R.D. a Retired Blacksmith	1a Carcinoma of Prostate Certified by R. E. Cooke M.D.	H. A. Beecroft Daughter 161. Watson Street Derby	Tenth July 1934	E Vernon Pratt Deputy Registrar.

I, E. Vernon Pratt Deputy Registrar of Births and Deaths for the Sub-District of Derby North West , in the County Borough of Derby
do hereby certify that this is a true copy of the Entry No. 424 in the Register Book of Deaths for the said Sub-District, and that such Register Book is now legally in my custody.

WITNESS MY HAND this 14th day of July , 19 34 .

E. Vernon Pratt Deputy Registrar of Births and Deaths

CAUTION.—Any person who (1) falsifies any of the particulars on this Certificate, or (2) uses it as true, knowing it to be falsified, is liable to Prosecution.

17

A. BEECROFT OF BLEASBY, NOTTINGHAMSHIRE (continued)

Document C: Certificate of Registry of Birth.

BIRTHS AND DEATHS REGISTRATION ACT, 1874.

CERTIFICATE of REGISTRY of BIRTH

I, the undersigned, Do hereby certify that the Birth of

Edith Mary Beecroft

born on the 26th *day of* Oct. 1903 *has been duly registered*

by me at Entry No. 472 *of the Register Book No.* 250

Witness my hand, this 9th *day of* Nov 19 03

{ *Registrar of Births and Deaths.*

_____ *District.* DERBY _____ *Sub-District.*

Note: The Edith Mary Beecroft mentioned in this document is known by the family to be the Edith Mary Beecroft recorded in the marriage licence (Document D).

A. BEECROFT OF BLEASBY, NOTTINGHAMSHIRE (continued)

Document D: Marriage Licence.

Harry Kevir Vaisey, one of His Majesty's Counsel, Master of Arts, Vicar General in Spirituals of the Right Reverend Father in God, **Alfred Edward John** by Divine Permission Lord Bishop of Derby, and Official Principal of the Episcopal and Consistorial Court of Derby TO OUR BELOVED IN CHRIST, Fred Valentine of the Parish of Saint Catherine Wigan in the County of Lancaster and Diocese of Liverpool a Bachelor of full age and Edith Mary Beecroft of the Parish of Saint Anne Derby in the County and Diocese of Derby a Spinster of full age Grace and Health. **Whereas** it is alleged that ye are desirous to proceed to the Solemnization of true and lawful Matrimony and **Whereas**

We being willing that these your desires may the more speedily obtain a due Effect and to the End thereof That this Marriage may be Publicly and lawfully Solemnized in the Parish Church of Saint Anne Derby aforesaid by the Rector, Vicar, or Curate thereof without the Publication or Proclamation of the Banns of Matrimony, **Provided** there shall appear no impediment in this case by reason of any former Marriage, Consanguinity, Affinity, or any other Cause whatsoever, nor any Suit Controversy or complaint be moved or now depending before any Judge, Ecclesiastical or Civil, for or by reason thereof. And likewise that the Celebration of this Marriage be had and done Publicly in the aforesaid Church between the hours of Eight in the forenoon and Six in the afternoon, **We** for lawful causes graciously **Grant** this our **Licence and Faculty** as well to you the Parties contracting as to the Rector, Vicar or Curate of the aforesaid Church who is designed to Solemnize the Marriage between you in the manner and form above specified according to the Rites of the Book of Common Prayer set forth for that purpose by the Authority of Parliament **Provided Always** that if in this case there shall hereafter appear any Fraud suggested to us or truth suppressed at the time of obtaining this Licence, then the Licence to be void and of no Effect in Law as if the same had never been granted, And in that case **We** inhibit all Ministers if anything of the Premises shall come to their knowledge, that they do not proceed to the Celebration of the said Marriage without consulting us.

Given under the Seal of our Office which we use in this behalf this Fifteenth day of November in the year of our Lord One Thousand Nine Hundred and Thirtyseven

Registrar.

Stat. 4 Geo. IV. c. 76, this Licence to continue in force only Three Months from the date hereof.

A. BEECROFT OF BLEASBY, NOTTINGHAMSHIRE (continued)

Document E: Factory and Workshop Certificate.

[THIS FORM of REQUISITION is furnished gratuitously. The applicant must fill in the required particulars in ink, sign his or her name at the foot, and either take the form to the SUPERIN-TENDENT REGISTRAR of the DISTRICT in which the Birth occurred, or send it to him, together with the fee of 6d. and 1d. for postage.]

The Form must NOT be sent to the Registrar-General.

The Certificate is not available for purposes of Secondary Education.

SCHEDULE.

THE FACTORY AND WORKSHOP ACT, 1901.

REQUISITION for a CERTIFIED COPY of an ENTRY of BIRTH for the purposes of the above-mentioned Act, or for any purpose connected with the EMPLOYMENT in LABOUR or ELEMENTARY EDUCATION of a Young Person under the age of Sixteen years, or of a Child.

To the **Superintendent Registrar** or **Registrar of Births and Deaths** having the custody of the Register in which the Birth of the under-mentioned Young Person or Child is registered:—

I, the undersigned, hereby demand, for the purpose mentioned below, a Certificate of the Birth of the Young Person or Child named in the subjoined Schedule.

Christian Name and Surname of the Young Person or Child of whose Age a Certificate is required.	Names of the Parents of such Young Person or Child.		Where such Young Person or Child was Born.	In what Year such Young Person or Child was Born.
	FATHER.	MOTHER.		
Fred Valentine	Henry	Eliz a.	Wigan	aug 1904

The Certificate is required for the following purpose, namely :—

Work

2.18
6+

Dated this _____ 28 _____ day of _____ July _____ 1917

Signature _____

Address _____

Occupation _____

WHEREAS by Section 134 of the Factory and Workshop Act, 1901, it is enacted as follows :—" Where the age of any young person under "the age of sixteen years, or child, is required to be ascertained or proved for the purposes of this Act, or for any purpose connected with the "employment in labour or elementary education of the young person or child, any person shall, on presenting a written requisition, in such "form, and containing such particulars as may be from time to time prescribed by the Local Government Board, and on payment of a fee of "sixpence, be entitled to obtain a certified copy under the hand of a registrar or superintendent registrar, of the entry in the register, under "the Births and Deaths Registration Acts, 1836 to 1874, of the birth of that young person or child ; and such form of requisition shall on "request be supplied without charge by every superintendent registrar and registrar of births, deaths, and marriages."   NOW THEREFORE, We, the Local Government Board, in pursuance of the powers given to Us by the Statutes in that behalf, hereby Order as follows :—

ARTICLE II.—The requisition to be made to entitle any person to obtain a certified copy of an entry of a registry of birth under the section

Note: The Fred Valentine mentioned in this document is known by the family to be the Fred Valentine recorded in the marriage licence (Document D).

A. BEECROFT OF BLEASBY, NOTTINGHAMSHIRE (continued)

Document F: Apprenticeship Indenture.

This Indenture Witnesseth, That William Beecroft son of Jane Beecroft of Lowdham in the County of Nottingham Widow as well of his own free will and consent as by and with the advice and consent of his said Mother doth put him self APPRENTICE to Thomas Haslam of Lowdham aforesaid Blacksmith

to learn his _____ _____ and with him _____ after the manner of an Apprentice to serve from the Tenth day of February _____ unto the full _____ _____ _____ _____ five _____ years, from thence next following; to be fully complete and ended; during which Term the said Apprentice h is said Master faithfully shall serve, his Secrets keep, h is lawful Commands every-where gladly do he shall do no Damage to h is said Master nor see it done by others, but to h is power shall let or forthwith give warning to h is said Master of the same; he shall not waste the goods of h is said Master nor give or lend them unlawfully to any; he shall neither buy nor sell without h is said Master's leave; Taverns, And Playhouses, he shall not haunt; at Cards, Dice Tables, or any other unlawful Games he shall not play; Matrimony he shall not contract; nor from the service of h is said Master Day or Night absent h im self; but in all things, as a faithful Apprentice he shall behave h im self towards h is said Master and all his Family, during the said Term. —AND the said Thomas Haslam

for and in consideration of the services of the said Apprentice to be faithfully rendered _____ the said Apprentice in the Art of a Blacksmith which he now useth, shall and will teach and instruct, in the best way and manner that he can ; and shall find unto the said Apprentice sufficient Meat, Drink, and Lodging, and _____ _____ during the said Term. And the said Jane Beecroft in consideration of the premises shall find into the said Apprentice during the said term all requisite and suitable clothes, washing, medicines and medical attendance and all other necessaries

AND for the true performance of all and every the said Covenants and Agreements, each of the said Parties bindeth him self unto the other firmly by these Presents. IN WITNESS whereof, the Parties aforesaid to these Indentures have hereunto interchangeably set their Hands and Seals the Twelfth Day of March in the forty fourth Year of the Reign of our Sovereign Lady Victoria, by the Grace of God, of the United Kingdom of Great Britain and Ireland, Queen, Defender of the Faith, and in the Year of our LORD One Thousand Eight Hundred and eighty-one

Sealed and delivered (being first duly
stamped) in the presence of }

William Beecroft

Jane Beecroft

Thos Haslam

John Pecock

Edwd Arthington

A. BEECROFT OF BLEASBY, NOTTINGHAMSHIRE (continued)

Document G: Electoral Roll for 161 Watson Street, Derby (King's Mead Ward).

1936

> Beecroft, Nicholas William
> Beecroft, Kathleen Annie
> Beecroft, Edith Mary

1937

> Beecroft, Kathleen Annie
> Beecroft, Edith Mary

1938

> Wright, Graham Alison
> Wright, Kathleen

A. BEECROFT OF BLEASBY, NOTTINGHAMSHIRE (continued)

Document G: Electoral Roll for 161 Watson Street, Derby (King's Mead Ward).

B. STEVENS OF BRATTON, WILTSHIRE

1851 Census Returns for Bratton, Wiltshire. (All entries for STEVENS and variants.)

Name	Relation to Head	Status	Age	Occupation	County Origin	Where Born
William Stevens	Head	Married	19	Ag Lab	Wilts	Bratton
Maria Stevens	Wife	Married	20		Wilts	Westbury
William Stevens	Head	Married	73	Ag Lab	Wilts	Dilton
Mary Stevens	Wife	Married	64		Wilts	East Lavington
Betsey Stevens	Dau	Unm	44	Wool Carder	Wilts	Bratton
George Stevens	Son	Unm	33	Ag Lab	Wilts	Bratton
Jane Flower	Lodger	Unm	52	Wool Carder	Wilts	Bratton
James Stevens	Head	Married	46	Farmer 20 ac	Wilts	Bratton
Rachel Stevens	Wife	Married	50	Wool Carder	Wilts	East Lavington
John Stevens	Son	Unm	18	Farmer's Son	Wilts	Bratton
Jane Stevens	Dau	Unm	14	Farmer's Dau	Wilts	Bratton
Ann Stevens	Dau		12	Scholar	Wilts	Bratton

Bratton Bishop's Transcripts. (All entries for STEVENS and variants.)

Baptisms 1829–1859

11 Jan	1835	James illegitimate s.o. Sarah Stevens
11 Jan	1835	John s.o. James and Ratchel Stevens of Bratton, labourer, born 19 Feb 1832
11 Jan	1835	William s.o. John and Ratchel Stevens of Bratton, labourer, born 19 Feb 1832
10 Jul	1836	James s.o. James and Rachel Stevens of Bratton, labourer
18 Mar	1838	Miriam d.o. of James Stephens, labourer
28 Apr	1839	Anne d.o. James Stephens, labourer

Burials 1835–1858

30 Jul	1838	Miriam d.o. James and Rachel Stephens, aged 3 months
30 Nov	1839	James s.o. Sarah Stephens, aged 4
3 Mar	1856	William Stevens, pauper aged 80

Marriages 1823–1831

Search negative

C. KNIGHT OF LONDON AND KENT

CERTIFIED COPY OF AN ENTRY OF BIRTH

GIVEN AT THE GENERAL REGISTER OFFICE

Application Number 3004885

REGISTRATION DISTRICT Wandsworth

BIRTH in the Sub-district of Clapham in the County of Surrey

No.	When and where born	Name, if any	Sex	Name and surname of father	Name, surname and maiden surname of mother	Occupation of father	Signature, description and residence of informant	When registered	Signature of registrar	Name entered after registration
251	Ninth October 1851 High Street	James Heekem	Boy	James Alexander Knight	Caroline Hough Knight formerly Heekem	Draper	Ja. Knight father High Street Clapham	Twenty seventh October 1851	James Firth Registrar	

CERTIFIED to be a true copy of an entry in the certified copy of a Register of Births in the District above mentioned.

Given at the GENERAL REGISTER OFFICE, under the Seal of the said office, the 16th day of May 19 72

BXBZ 249205

*See note overleaf

CAUTION: It is an offence to falsify a certificate or to make or knowingly use a false certificate or a copy of a false certificate intending it to be accepted as genuine to the prejudice of any person or to possess a certificate knowing it to be false without lawful authority.

24

C. KNIGHT OF LONDON AND KENT (continued)

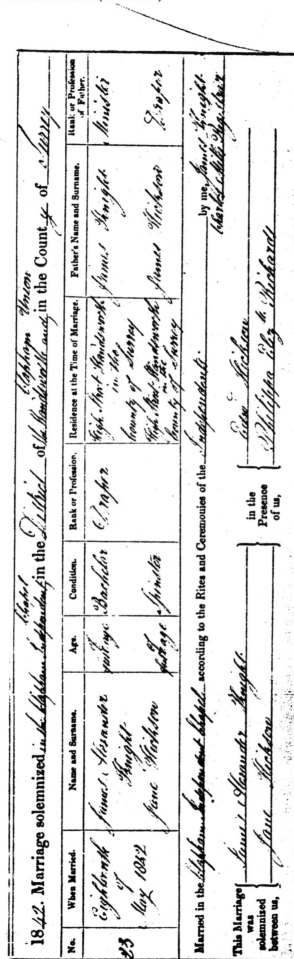

CERTIFIED COPY OF AN ENTRY OF MARRIAGE GIVEN AT THE GENERAL REGISTER OFFICE, LONDON

Application Number. B14432

18_42_. Marriage solemnized in the Clapham Independent Chapel in the District of Wandsworth and in the County of Surrey

No.	When Married.	Name and Surname.	Age.	Condition.	Rank or Profession.	Residence at the Time of Marriage.	Father's Name and Surname.	Rank or Profession of Father.
93	Eighteenth of May 1842	Samuel Alexander Knight	full age	Bachelor	Draper	High Street Wandsworth in the County of Surrey	James Knight	Minister
		Jane Nickson	full age	Spinster		High Street Wandsworth in the County of Surrey	James Nickson	Draper

Married in the Clapham Independent Chapel according to the Rites and Ceremonies of the Independent by me, James Knight, Charles Mills Registrar.

This Marriage was solemnized between us, { Samuel Alexander Knight / Jane Nickson } in the Presence of us, { Eliza Nickson / Philippa Eliz A. Nickson }

MX 012192

CERTIFIED to be a true copy of an entry in the certified copy of a register of Marriages in the Registration District of Wandsworth & Clapham

Given at the GENERAL REGISTER OFFICE, LONDON, under the Seal of the said Office, the 17th day of April 19 86

The certificate is issued in pursuance of section 65 of the Marriage Act 1949. Sub-section 3 of that section provides that any certified copy of an entry purporting to be sealed or stamped with the seal of the General Register Office shall be received as evidence of the marriage to which it relates without any further or other proof of the entry, and no certified copy purporting to have been given in the said Office shall be of any force or effect unless it is sealed or stamped as aforesaid.

CAUTION:—It is an offence to falsify a certificate or to make or knowingly use a false certificate or a copy of a false certificate in ending it to be accepted as genuine to the prejudice of any person, or to possess a certificate knowing it to be false without lawful authority.

Dd 8923942 70M 9/85 Mcr(731104)

Form A5 MX

25

C. KNIGHT OF LONDON AND KENT (continued)

This is the last Will and Testament of me
The Reverend James Knight of Deal in the County of Kent Minister
of the Gospel I direct that all my just debts funeral and testamentary
expences and Legacies may be paid as soon as conveniently may be after
my decease *I give* and devise All those my two Messuages or Tenements in
the Sheds Buildings Land and Appurtenances to the same respectively
belonging situate at Kingston upon Thames in the County of Surrey and
now or late in the several occupations of   Wilson and   Lind
To the use of my Son David Knight his Heirs and Assigns for ever I give
and devise All that my other Messuage or Tenement with the Buildings la
and Appurtenances thereunto belonging situate at Kingston upon Thames upo
in the said County of Surrey and now or late in the occupation of
Gibbs To the use of my Son James Alexander Knight his Heirs and Assigns fo
ever I give and bequeath to each of them The Reverend Henry John Rook
Faversham in the County of Kent Minister of the Gospel and Edmund Brown
Deal in the said County of Kent Gentleman / my Executors hereinafter named
the sum of Five Pounds I give devise and bequeath all the rest residue a
remainder of my real Estate and also of my Goods Chattels Monies Securitie
for Money and other my personal Estate and Effects of what nature and kin
soever and wheresoever unto and to the use of my said Son James Alexander
Knight his Heirs Executors Administrators and Assigns for ever And I app
the said Henry John Rook and Edmund Brown Executors of this my Will
In witness whereof I the said James Knight (the Testator) have to this r
last Will and Testament set my hand this eleventh day of July One thousa
eight hundred and sixty one ——— *James Knight* ———
Signed by the said James Knight (the Testator) as and for his last W
and Testament in the presence of us, present at the same time, who here
at his request in his presence and in the presence of each other attest a
subscribe the same accordingly ——— R. Joynes Emmerson Sol. San
James Moat Clerk to Mess. Surrage & Emmerson Sol. Sandwic

I James Knight of Deal in the County of Kent Minister
the Gospel do hereby declare this to be a Codicil to my aforegoing W
Whereas I have for many years past been a Member of the Protest
Union Society And whereas I have by my said Will given and

C. KNIGHT OF LONDON AND KENT (continued)

bequeathed all my Monies Securities for Money and other my
personal Estate and Effects of what nature and kind soever and wheresoever
unto my Son James Alexander Knight his Executors Administrators and
Assigns Now I do hereby revoke the said bequest so far as the same
extends to the Monies which shall become payable upon my decease
from the same Society And I give and bequeath all and singular
the same Monies to become due and payable upon my decease from the
said Society ~~~~~~~~~~ as aforesaid unto my Son
David Knight his Executors Administrators and Assigns absolutely
And in all other respects I confirm my said Will In witness whereof
I the said James Knight (the Testator) have to this Codicil set my
hand this sixth day of August One thousand eight hundred and
sixty one —— James Knight —— Signed by the said
James Knight (the Testator) as and for a Codicil to his said Will in
the presence of us (present at the same time) who hereby at his request
in his presence and in the presence of each other attest and subscribe
the same accordingly —— R. Joynes Emmerson Solr Sandwich
Benjn Dixson Commander in the Royal Navy Deal.

On the 30th day of May 1864 the Will with one Codicil
thereto of. The Reverend James Knight late of Deal in the
County of Kent Minister of the Gospel was proved by the
Oaths of Henry John Rook and Edmund Brown the Executors
named in the Will having been first sworn duly to administer

Effects under £600
Probate extracted by
Surrage & Emmerson
Solrs Sandwich

C. KNIGHT OF LONDON AND KENT (continued)

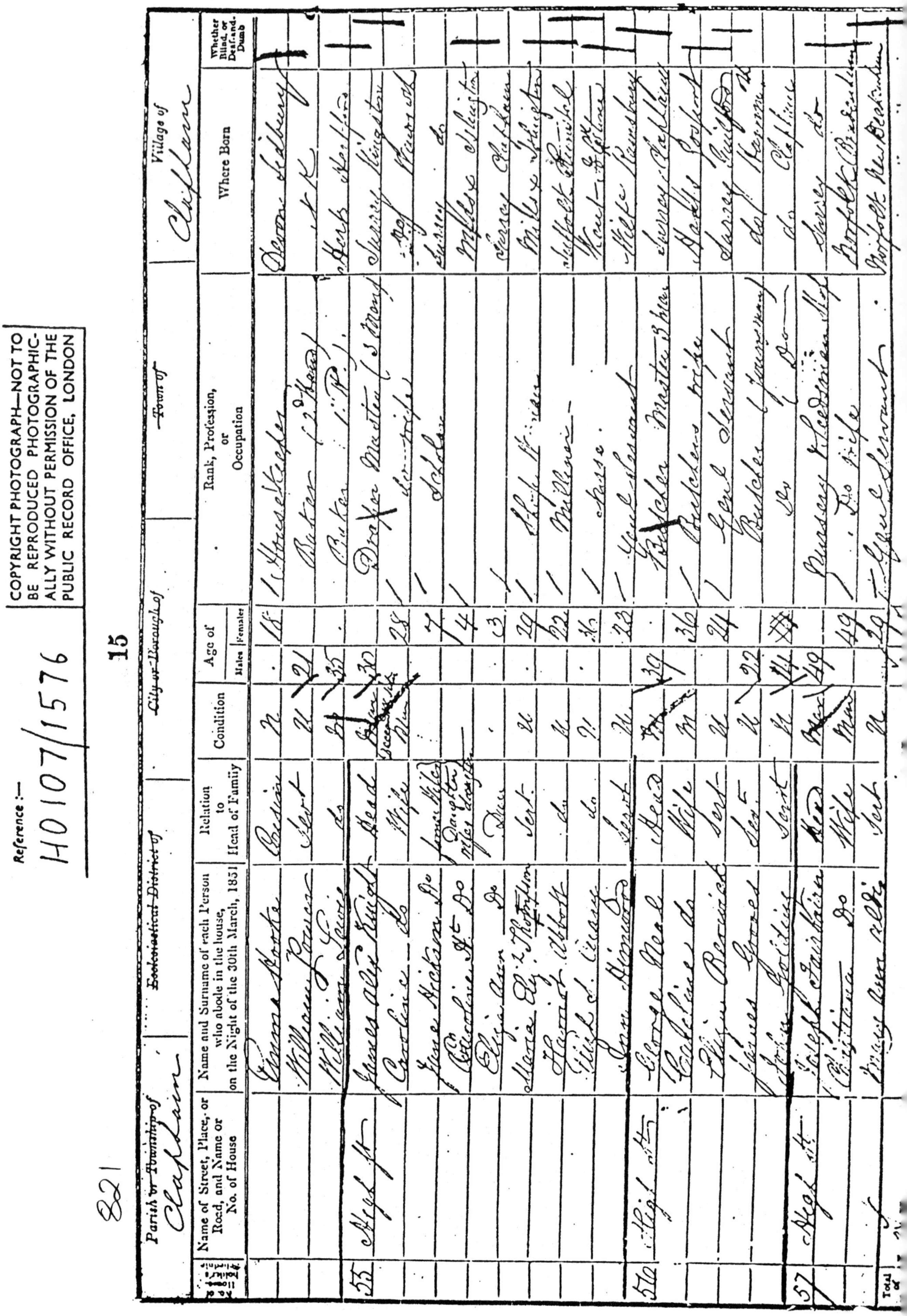

Reference :— HO107/1576

821

15

Parish ~~or Township~~ of Clapham | ~~Ecclesiastical District of~~ | ~~City or Borough of~~ | ~~Town of~~ | Village of Clapham

No. of Householder's Schedule	Name of Street, Place, or Road, and Name or No. of House	Name and Surname of each Person who abode in the house, on the Night of the 30th March, 1851	Relation to Head of Family	Condition	Age of Males	Age of Females	Rank, Profession, or Occupation	Where Born	Whether Blind, or Deaf-and-Dumb
		Emma Hooke	Cousin	U		18	Housekeeper	Devon Sidbury	
		William Power	Servt	U	21		Baker (2d Hand)	N K	
		William Lewis	do	U	35		Baker (Pt)	Herts Hertford	
55	High St	James Alex Knight	Head	Mar	30		Draper Master (3 Men)	Surrey Kingston	
		Caroline do	Wife	Mar		28	do wife	Notts Worksop	
		Jane Hickson Do	[illegible]			7	Scholar	Surrey do	
		Caroline Ht Do	Daughter			4		Middx Islington	
		Eliza Ann Do	Dau			3		Surrey Clapham	
		Maria Eliz Thompson	Servt	U		29	Shopwoman	Middx Islington	
		Harriot Abbott	do	U		22	Milliner	Suffolk [illegible]	
		[illegible]	do	U		36	Nurse	Kent [illegible]	
		Ann Himwood	Servt	U		23	Genl Servant	Wilts Ramsbury	
56	High St	George Neal	Head	M	39		Butcher Master 3 Men	Surrey Clapham	
		Caroline do	Wife	M		36	Butchers wife	Hants Gosport	
		Eliza Berwick	Servt	U		24	Genl Servant	Surrey Guilford	
		James Groves	Servt	U	22		Butcher (Journeyman)	do Hammersmith	
		John Golding	Servt	U	14		do (Do)	do Clapham	
57	High St	Joseph Fairbairn	Head	Mar	49		Nursery & Seedsman Shop	Surrey do	
		Christiana Do	Wife	Mar		49	Do wife	Norfolk Brakendale	
		Mary Ann Aldis	Servt	U		29	Genl Servant	Norfolk New Buckenham	

D. PARSLER OF TETSWORTH, OXFORDSHIRE

CERTIFIED COPY OF AN ENTRY OF MARRIAGE

Given at the GENERAL REGISTER OFFICE, LONDON

Application Number G 35512

Registration District Thame

1867. Marriage solemnized at by Banns

in the church of Tetsworth in the County of Oxford

No.	(1) When married	(2) Name and Surname	(3) Age	(4) Condition	(5) Rank or profession	(6) Residence at the time of marriage	(7) Father's name and surname	(8) Rank or profession of father
80	Sept 16th	John Parsler	27	Bachelor	Mason	Tetsworth	James Parsler	Mason
		Mary Hawes	30	Spinster	Servant	Tetsworth	William Hawes	Groom

Married in the Church of Tetsworth according to the Rites and Ceremonies of the Church of England by me

This marriage was solemnized between us, { John Parsler / Mary Hawes } in the presence of us, { The mark of x Thomas Hawes / Ann Parsler } I W Pools Vicar

CERTIFIED to be a true copy of an entry in the certified copy of a Register of Marriages in the District above mentioned.

Given at the GENERAL REGISTER OFFICE, LONDON, under the Seal of the said Office, the 13th day of January 1989

MB 381182

D. PARSLER OF TETSWORTH, OXFORDSHIRE (continued)

[Page 15] 65

The undermentioned Houses are situate within the Boundaries of the

No. of Schedule	ROAD, STREET, &c., and No. or NAME of HOUSE	HOUSES Inhabited	NAME and Surname of each Person	RELATION to Head of Family	CONDITION as to Marriage	AGE last Birthday Males / Females	Rank, Profession, or OCCUPATION	WHERE BORN	If (1) Deaf-and-Dumb (2) Blind (3) Imbecile or Idiot (4) Lunatic
64	3 Commercial Rd	1	John Parsler	Head	Mar	44	Bricklayer	Oxon, Tetsworth	
			Mary do	Wife	Mar			do	
			Mary do	Dau	Unm	13	Scholar	do	
			Alice do	Dau		8	do	do	
			Herbert R. do	Son		6	do	do	
65	do	1	George Linden	Head	Mar	70	Agricul. Labourer	Buck, Nottingham	
			Sarah do	Wife	Mar	27		do Tetsworth	
			Kate do	Dau		5	Scholar	do	
			Frederick do	Son		3	do	do	
			Anna do	Dau		1		Oxon Tetsworth	
66	do	1	William Arnott	Head	Mar	44	Agricul. Labourer	do do	
			Mary do	Wife	Mar	37		do do	
			Mary do	Dau		9	Scholar	do do	
			George do	Son		7	do	do do	
			Walt do	Son		5		do do	
			Louisa Parsler			1		do do	
67	do	1	William Briningham	Head	Mar	37	Bricklayer	do Great Haseley	
			Jacob do	Wife	Mar	25	Postman & Farmer	do Tetsworth	
			Etta Cox	Son		4		do Great Milton	
			Amy do	Son		2		do Tetsworth	
68	do	1	Henry Kidwell	Head	Mar	66	Farmer of 15 acre	do Cortley	
			Elizabeth do	Wife	Mar	57		do Tetsworth	
			Daniel E. do	Son		30		do Great Milton	

| | Total of Houses... 5 | | Total of Males and Females | | | 10 | |

D. PARSLER OF TETSWORTH, OXFORDSHIRE (continued)

Tetsworth, Oxfordshire. Transcript of Parish Registers. (All entries for PARSLER and variants.)

Baptisms 1750–1880

22	May	1836	Sarah Ann Parslow d.o. James and Mary, mason
11	Feb	1838	James Parsler s.o. James and Mary, bricklayer
11	Feb	1838	Elizabeth Parsler d.o. James and Mary, bricklayer
25	Dec	1840	John Parsler s.o. James and Mary, lab
19	Feb	1843	Ann Paisler d.o. James and Mary, mason
8	Jun	1845	Thomas Paisler s.o. James and Mary, mason
28	Feb	1847	Jane Parsler d.o. James and Mary, mason
7	Jun	1852	Emma Parsler d.o. James and Mary, mason
7	Jun	1852	Thomas Parsler s.o. James and Mary, mason
9	Apr	1855	Mary Parslow d.o. James and Mary, mason

Marriages 1750–1860

17	Oct	1827	Parsler James, bachelor of Haseley
			Franklin Mary, wid
			wit Eliza Parsler, James Fleet Shrimpton
11	Jul	1835	Parsler James, widr
			Harris Mary, sp
			wit Thomas White, Martha Harris

Burials 1750–1895

31	Mar	1846	Parsler Thomas 10 mth
5	Apr	1855	Parslow Mary 40
19	Apr	1855	Parslow Mary 2 wks
2	Nov	1859	Parslee Thomas 7 yrs
17	Jul	1885	Parsler James 84

E. BAYLIS OF KEMPSEY, WORCESTERSHIRE

Kempsey, Worcestershire, Parish Registers. (All entries for BAYLIS and variants.)

Baptisms 1785–1825

3	Oct	1800	Robert s.o. Robert and Mary Baylis
15	Jun	1802	James s.o. Robert Bayliss, yeoman of Norman Common
23	Nov	1806	Henry s.o. Robert and Mary Baylis
2	Aug	1808	Elizabeth d.o. Robert and Mary Baylis
17	Feb	1811	Mary d.o. Robert and Mary Baylis

Marriages 1785–1825

16 Jun 1805   Robert Baylis married Mary Barnes botp by licence, both signed their names.
Witnessed Henry Carpenter and Ann Harris.

Census Return for Kempsey. (All entries for BAYLIS and variants.)

	Name	Age	Occupation	Born in County?
Norman Common	Mary Baylies	55	Laundress	Yes
	Anne Baylies	35	Ironer	No
	Henry Baylies	35	Ag. Lab.	Yes
	Elizabeth Baylies	30	Laundress	Yes
	Robert Parker	12	Ag. Lab.	Yes

E. BAYLIS OF KEMPSEY, WORCESTERSHIRE (continued)

ID 922071

The statutory fee for this certificate is 3s. 9d.
Where a search is necessary to find the entry,
a search fee is payable in addition.

(Printed by authority of the Registrar General.)

D. Cert.
R.B.D.

CERTIFIED COPY of an ENTRY OF DEATH
Pursuant to the Births and Deaths Registration Act, 1953

Registration District   Worcester

1838.   Death in the Sub-district of   Worcester   in the County of Worcester

No.	When and where died	Name and surname	Sex	Age	Occupation	Cause of death	Signature, description, and residence of informant	When registered	Signature of registrar
361	9th Feb 1838 Norman Common Kempsey	Robert Baylis	Male	60 yrs	Yeoman	Injuries resulting from accidental burning	Certificate from R. Pugh Coroner for the city of Worcester after inquest held 10 Feb 1838	11 Feb 1838	C. B. Owen. Registrar.

I, P. D. Sandman, Registrar of Births and Deaths for the Sub-district of Worcester, in the County of Worcester do hereby certify that this is a true copy of Entry No. 421 in the Register Book of Deaths for the said Sub-district, and that such Register Book is now legally in my custody.

WITNESS MY HAND this 5th day of July, 1991.

Registrar of Births and Deaths.

CAUTION.—Any person who (1) falsifies any of the particulars on this certificate, or (2) uses a falsified certificate as true, knowing it to be false, is liable to prosecution.

33

E. BAYLIS OF KEMPSEY, WORCESTERSHIRE (continued)

I, Robert Baylis of Norman Common in the parish of Kempsey in the County of Worcester do make this my last Will and Testament, I give & devise unto my Wife Mary Baylis all the little Property I am possessed of, the Cottage built by me situate lying & being on the Border of Norman Common with the Garden adjoining, to have & to hold to her & her heirs & assigns for ever, & also all the furniture in the said Cottage, & all the Vegetables in the said Garden & all the Money I may be possessed of at my decease, to be enjoyed by her as long as she may live — If, however, she may not wish to sell the said Cottage & Garden to provide for her maintenance during her natural life, It is my Will that the said Cottage & Garden be sold at her decease & Equally divided between my five children Robert Baylis, James Baylis, Henry Baylis, Elizabeth Baylis, & Mary Parker & that all my Household Furniture be equally divided between my two Daughters Elizabeth Baylis & Mary Parker, & I appoint my said Wife Mary Baylis Executrix of this my Will, In Witness whereof, I the said Testator Robert Baylis have set my hand & seal this

E. BAYLIS OF KEMPSEY, WORCESTERSHIRE (continued)

F. OUGH OF QUETHIOCK, CORNWALL

1841 Census Returns for Quethiock, Cornwall (All entries for OUGH or variants.)

Name	Age	Occupation	Born in County
Trenance			
Charles Ough	20	Mason	Yes
Quethiock Village			
James Ough	30	Mason	Yes
Eliza Ough	25		Yes
Sophia Ough	5		Yes
Catherine Ough	2		Yes
Charlotte Ough	1		Yes
William Ough	60	Mason	Yes
Ann Ough	60		Yes
John Ough	25	Mason	Yes

Quethiock Parish Registers. (All entries for OUGH or variants.)

Baptisms 1800–1855

2 Jan	1809	James s.o. William and Ann Ough	
15 Apr	1814	Sarah d.o. William and Ann Ough, mason of Churchtown, Quethiock	
3 Oct	1818	Charles s.o. William and Ann Ough, mason of Churchtown, Quethiock	
13 Sep	1836	Sophia base-born d.o. James Ough and Eliza Rowe, mason of Quethiock	
10 Dec	1839	Charlotte d.o. James and Eliza Ough, mason of Quethiock	

Marriages 1820–1855

8 Jan 1836   John Ough, bachelor of this parish married Ellen Rowe of Sheviock by banns.
Witnesses James Ough and Eliza Rowe.

25 Jul 1837   James Ough, bachelor, aged 28, Mason of Quethiock, s.o. William Ough, mason. Married by banns to Eliza Rowe, spinster, aged 22, of Sheviock, father not known.
Witnesses John and Ellen Ough.

Burials 1837–1855

4 May	1838	Ellen Ough of Sheviock aged 25
23 Feb	1843	John Ough of Sheviock aged 30
2 Apr	1852	William Ough of Churchtown, Quethiock aged 73

F. OUGH OF QUETHIOCK, CORNWALL (continued)

I William Ough of Quethiock in the County of Cornwall (Mason) do make my last Will and Testament in manner following. First I Give and bequeath unto my Four Children James, Lovdy, Sarah and William Ough all the Public House, Garden, Stable [. . . . .] equally Shared among them. Secondly I give and bequeath unto my son Charles Ough all that Dwelling House and Pig house situated near to or adjoining the Public House, now in my own occupation, I Give unto James my son my Hanging Press now in my Possession. I Give unto Lovdy my Daughter my Large Clothes Chest now in [. . . . .] I Give unto [. . . . . . .] my daughter my [. . . . .] in my possession. I Give unto William my son my Clock now in my possession. I Give unto Charles my son my Bed and Bedding now in my possession also my Chest of Drawers (and [. . .] being in my possession, and I give and bequeath unto all my Children (to be equally divided among them all) my other Goods Chattles [. . . . .] [. . . . .] wheresoever situated nothing in to [. . .] ned in this my Will. Also I give unto Ann Ough my Wife the sum of Eight Pounds Per year so long as she shall live, to be paid Her Yearly or otherwise as she may require after my decease

F. OUGH OF QUETHIOCK, CORNWALL (continued)

from the Rents arising from the Property which I now bequeath unto my Children, That is to Say One Pound Twelve shillings to be paid Her Annually, or otherwise as she may require from each of my Five Children, I also Give unto George Snell Son of my Daughter Loveday the Sum of Five pound to be paid Him at my Death out of the money that will be due to me from the Death Club at Liskeard, And lastly, it is my Will that the Remainder of the money of the Liskeard Club together with that of Quethiock Club shall be equally divided among all my Children together with Ann Ough my Wife, First deducting all reasonable expences for my Funeral out of it and also for Ann Ough my Wife to have the management of my Funeral Expenses,

And I hereby nominate and appoint James and William Ough my Sons, Executors of this my last Will and Testament,

Witness my Hand this Twenty Seventh day of September in the Year of our Lord One Thousand Eight Hundred and Fifty One

William ough

Signed by the said Testator in the presence of us who in his presence, and in the presence of each other have hereunto Subscribed our names as Witnesses

Samuel Rogers

Robert H Greet

38

G. BARROW OF WOOLASTONE, GLOUCESTERSHIRE

Woolastone, Gloucestershire, Parish Registers. (All entries for BARROW and variants.)

Baptisms, Marriages and Burials 1740–1800

8 Jul	1743	John, s.o. Mr John Barrow and Mrs Francis, bap
16 Aug	1743	John, s.o. Mr John Barrow, buried
22 Nov	1744	Francis, d.o. Mr John Barraw and Francis, bap
12 Jun	1746	John, s.o. John and Fransis Barrow, bap
14 Nov	1748	Richard, s.o. John and Francis Barrow, bap
30 Jun	1752	Ms Frances ye wife of Mr John Barrow, buried
20 Mar	1757	Ms Elizabeth ye wife of Mr John Barrow, buried
2 Jun	1773	John, s.o. Rich'd Barrow and Helen, bap
12 Feb	1775	Sarah, d.o. Rich'd and Helen Barrow, bap
14 Dec	1775	John Barrow, buried
19 Mar	1777	John, s.o. John and Love Barrow, bap
1 Apr	1777	John, s.o. John and Love Barrow, buried
3 May	1777	Richard Barrow, buried
8 Jun	1778	John, s.o. John and Love Barrow, bap
1 Feb	1780	Richard Barrow an infant, buried
16 May	1780	Elizabeth, d.o. John and Love Barrow, bap
5 Nov	1781	Sarah Barrow an infant, buried, privately baptized
13 Oct	1782	Richard, s.o. John and Love Barrow, bap
25 Jul	1784	James Barrow, buried
5 Sep	1784	John Barrow, Senr., buried
11 May	1785	Love, the wife of John Barrow, buried
31 Jul	.1785	James, s.o. John and Love Barrow, bap
19 Mar	1787	James, s.o. John and Love Barrow, buried

Woolastone Monumental Inscriptions (from Bigland's Gloucestershire Collections)

In Memory of / LOVE BARROW, wife of / JOHN BARROW, of Woollaston Grange, / who died 18 May 1785, / Aged 37 Years /

Here lies interred the body of / ANN, the wife of WALTER HARRIS, / Daughter of RICHARD BARROW, / Gent. She died 20 Oct 1786, Aged 73 Years./
In Memory of / WILLIAM HARRIS, Gent., / Sail Maker, of this Parish, / who died 29 June 1799, / Aged 65 Years. / In Memory of / EDWARD WHITE, of this parish, / who died the 18 of October 1787, / Aged 51 Years. / Also MARY, Widow of the above / EDWARD WHITE, and Relict of / RICHARD HARRIS, tanner, / of this Parish, who died / Sept 16, 1792, Aged 63 Years. / SARAH, the daughter of / JOHN and MARY SADLER, / who died Aged 3 days. / In memory of / RICHARD BARROW, Gent., / who died 23 June 1720. / MARY, the daughter of RICHARD / BARROW, and wife of GEORGE / BUCKLE, who died 12 Decr 1733. / GEORGE, the Son of GEORGE and / MARY BUCKLE, who died the / 16 of Novr 1773. Aged 87 Years. / JOHN BARROW, Gent. / who departed this life, / 12 Decr 1775, Aged 77 Years./

G. BARROW OF WOOLASTONE, GLOUCESTERSHIRE (continued)

Transcript of the Will of JOHN BARROW, High Woolastone, Gloucestershire, 1785

In the Name of God Amen, I, JOHN BARROW of High Woollastone in the County of Gloucester, Gentleman, of sound and disposing Mind, Memory and Understanding, do Pronounce and declare my last Will and Testament in manner following. All and Singular my Goods, Chattels Furniture of Household, Stock of Corn Grain, hay, Implements of Husbandry, cattle, etc., which did belong to Mrs. SARAH HAMMOND, late of High Wollastone deceased and which were bequeathed to me in her last Will and Testament, I give and bequeath unto SELWYN JAMES of the Town of Chepstow in the County of Monmouth, Esquire, and JAMES HAMMOND of Brookend in the Parish of Wollastone in the County of Glocester, Tanner, In Trust that they shall thereout pay the several legacies charged there upon by the said SARAH HAMMOND in and by her last will and Testament to the several Persons therein mentioned, and after the payment thereof any part remaining to permit my daughter FRANCES now wife of WILLIAM WILLIAMS to have the use and profits therof for her natural life for her own sole use and Benefit. And from the decease of my said Daughter FRANCES Upon Trust that they the said SELWYN JAMES and JAMES HAMMOND shall sell and dispose of the said Stock goods, chattels and effects for the most Money that can be got for the same and pay the monies arising amongst JOHN, HENRY, FRANCES, SARAH, MARY and RICHARD, children of my said Daughter FRANCES by the said WILLIAM WILLIAMS, share and share alike, at their respective ages of Twenty one years or the day or days of their Marriage. All and singular my freehold and leasehold several messuages, lands, tenements, Hereditaments and premises whatsoever, situate in the Tything of Aylburton in the Parish of Lydney and in the several Parishes of Lydney, Alvington, Wollastone and Tidenham or else where, I give, devise and bequeath unto my son JOHN BARROW of Wollastone Grange in the County of Glocester, Gentleman, his heirs, executors, administrators and assigns for ever. And also all my Goods, Chattels, Household Furniture, farming and other Stock of Cattle, Grain, Hay, etc., and all other my Personal Estate and Effects I Give and bequeath unto my said son JOHN BARROW, his executors, etc., for ever, charged with the payment of one clear yearly annuity of Fifteen Pounds unto my said Daughter FRANCES for the term of her natural Life, to and for her own sole and separate use, and from and after her decease, charged with the payment of the sum of Three hundred Pounds to and amongst the said JOHN, HENRY, FRANCES, SARAH, MARY and RICHARD WILLIAMS, the children of the said FRANCES, And also charged with the payment of the sum of One Hundred and Twenty Pounds to the before mentioned six children of the said FRANCES WILLIAMS, and also charged with the payment of Thirty pounds apiece to the Three Children of my son RICHARD at their respective ages of twenty one years or the day or days of their Marriage.

I appoint my said son JOHN BARROW Sole Executor of this my Will.
Dated this 7th October 1782.

Witnesses   THOMAS EVANS
            MARY WILLIAMS
            (illegible) DAVIES

Proved 9th March 1785 by JOHN BARROW, the son and sole executor.

H. MUFFET OF ST COLUMB MINOR, CORNWALL

St Columb Minor, Cornwall, Parish Registers. (All entries for Muffet and variants.)

Baptisms 1675–1752

25	Feb	1675/6	John s.o. Adam Muffet
8	Jun	1678	Adam s.o. Adam Mouffett
28	Feb	1679/80	William s.o. Adam Mouffett
30	Sep	1682	Jane d.o. Adam Moffett
28	Dec	1684	Ann d.o. Adam Muffett
14	Aug	1687	Robert s.o. Adam Moffett
20	Apr	1690	Mary and Elizabeth twaines unto Adam Muffett
11	Nov	1700	Adam s.o. John and Elizabeth Muffett
29	May	1703	Richard s.o. John and Elizabeth Muffett
24	Feb	1705/6	Elizabeth d.o. John and Elizabeth Muffett
4	Sep	1709	Mary d.o. John and Elizabeth Muffett
9	May	1713	John s.o. John and Elizabeth Muffett

Burials 1675–1752

4	Jun	1686	William s.o. Adam Muffett
25	Jun	1689	Robert s.o. Adam Muffett
23	Apr	1690	Elizabeth d.o. Adam Muffett
4	Jun	1690	Mary d.o. Adam Muffett
18	Aug	1692	Adam Muffett
15	Jul	1726	Mary d.o. John Muffett
3	Aug	1726	Brigit Muffet, widow
19	Aug	1740	John Moffatt
24	Jul	1752	Elizabeth Moffat, widow

Marriages 1675–1752

| 23 | Oct | 1675 | Adam Moffat and Brigit Glandfield |
| 2 | Dec | 1699 | John Muffett and Elizabeth Stone |

H. MUFFET OF ST COLUMB MINOR, CORNWALL (continued)

In the name of god (Amen) John Muffat of the parish of St Columb
minor in the County of Cornwall yeoman booing Sick & weake
but of good and perfect mind & memory thanks boo unto Allmighty
god, And calling to mind the many of to Sins and Transgressions
of this transitory Life I doo Recomend my Soul in to the hand
of Allmighty god and my Body to boo decently buryed Accordin
to the disscretion of my Executors in manor and forme of a wth

Item I give unto my Son Adam one ffeather Bed furnished
Item I give unto my Son Richard my Land in Trenick to him and his
heirs for Ever, to Possess the Same at or within three
years After my Decease

and the sd. Richd. Muff to pay to his mother Elizabeth Muff
yearly out of the sd. Land the Sume of ffive pounds
During her Natturall life, and the Hall Chamber as a lodg
During her life

Item I oblidg my sd Son Richd to pay all of the above sd
the Sume of two hundred pounds, two wards Depts and
Legacys

Item I give my wife the Bed furnished over the Halle and one
brass Crock the midle most two Spits Slates two platers and on
In Ocking Chest

Item I give my Daughter Elizabeth the Sume of fifty pounds to boo
payd her at or within the Compass of the my Decease one Bed furnish
and one hanging Press

Item I give my Daughter Bridget the Sume of ffifty pounds to boo
payd her at the Age of twenty one, But to Receive Interest for
the Same at or Immediatly after my Decease with a Bed furn

Item I give my Daugh Jane fifty pounds to boo payd her at the Age of
twenty But to Receive Interest for the Same at or Immedeatly
after my Decease with a Bed furnisht

Item I give my sd Son or Chattle Estate in Nuckey now in my Poss
the Lands of the Right honurable Lord, Erle of Radnor and on
Chattle Estate now In my Possession within the Village of
Trenick booing the Lands of the Esqr. Clubery

H. MUFFET OF ST COLUMB MINOR, CORNWALL (continued)

Itt I do herby Conftate and appoynt my well beloued wife to bee
my hole and folle Executrix of this my last will and Testement
Revoking and Diffanouling all other will or wills of what
nature or kind So Euer In witnefs wher of I have vnto fett
my hand and Seall this 17th Day of April Annoq Domini 1731

Teft Ruth Pecoe

Willm Piffoe

John Moffatt

Memo: If the Sd John Muffatt Effects do not hold out to pay the Depts
and Legaciis then the Eftate of Chette in howkay now the Lands
of Ineston Poll amounto, is to bee Sold, otherwayes I do Solle the
Sd tenem on my Sone Iohn by him To bee Enjoyd during the Tearm
there on

I. JESSON OF HALIFAX, YORKSHIRE AND COSTON, LEICESTERSHIRE

Alumni Cantabrigienses 1752–1900

JESSON, WILLIAM. Adm. pens. at St John's Oct. 5, 1864. S. of William, Excise Officer [and Mary]. B. Mar. 13, 1838, at Pontefract, Yorks. Bapt. Apr. 8, 1838. School, Maida Hill. Matric. Michs. 1864; B.A. 1868; M.A. 1875. Ord. deacon (Ripon) 1870; priest (Bishop Ryan, for Ripon)1871; C. of Allerton Bywater, Yorks., 1870-3. C. of Liverpool, 1873-5. V. of Ditton, Lancs., 1875-8. C. of Stoneham, Hants., 1878-80. C. of Diptford, Devon, 1880-2, V. of Mickley, Northumb., 1882-3.
Disappears from *Crockford* 1894.

Coston, Leicestershire, Parish Registers (All entries for JESSON or variants.)

Baptisms 1800–1812

22	Apr	1801	William s.o. John and Ann Jesson
11	Apr	1806	John s.o. John and Ann Jesson
16	Sep	1810	Jane d.o. John and Ann Jesson
27	Dec	1812	Mary Ann d.o. John and Ann Jesson

I. JESSON OF HALIFAX, YORKSHIRE (continued)

CERTIFIED COPY OF AN ENTRY OF BIRTH

GIVEN AT THE GENERAL REGISTER OFFICE, LONDON.

Application Number R24056

BIRTH in the Sub-district of Pontefract **in the** County of York

REGISTRATION DISTRICT Pontefract

1838

No.	When and where born	Name, if any	Sex	Name, and surname of father	Name, surname, and maiden surname of mother	Occupation of father	Signature, description and residence of informant	When registered	Signature of registrar	Name entered after registration
Columns:—	1	2	3	4	5	6	7	8	9	10*
203	Thirteenth of March 1838 Parish of Pontefract	William	Boy	William Jesson	Mary Jesson formerly Hustwick	Exciseman	Wm Jesson father, 1 Horsefair Pontefract	Twenty eighth of March 1838	Edward Dyson Registrar	

*See note overleaf.

CERTIFIED to be a true copy of an entry in the certified copy of a Register of Births in the District above mentioned.
Given at the GENERAL REGISTER OFFICE, LONDON, under the Seal of the said Office, the 28th day of February 1985.

BCA 094264

Form A502 Dd.8343773 30M 7/84 Mcr(304696)

I. JESSON OF HALIFAX, YORKSHIRE (continued)

CERTIFIED COPY OF AN ENTRY OF DEATH

GIVEN AT THE GENERAL REGISTER OFFICE, LONDON

Application Number B 34965

REGISTRATION DISTRICT Halifax

1864. DEATH in the Sub-district of Halifax in the County of York

No.	When and Where died	Name and surname	Sex	Age	Occupation	Cause of death	Signature, description and residence of informant	When registered	Signature of registrar
Columns:— 1	2	3	4	5	6	7	8	9
468	Sixteenth May 1864 2 High Street Halifax	William Jesson	Male	63 yars	Supervisor Inland Revenue	Softening of the Brain (supernummerated, certified)	William Jesson In attendance 2 High Street Halifax	Nineteenth May 1864	Hy. Leach Registrar

CERTIFIED to be a true copy of an entry in the certified copy of a Register of Deaths in the District above mentioned.
Given at the GENERAL REGISTER OFFICE, LONDON, under the Seal of the said Office, the 20th day of March 19 85

This certificate is issued in pursuance of the Births and Deaths Registration Act 1953. Section 34 provides that any certified copy of an entry purporting to be sealed or stamped with the seal of the General Register Office shall be received as evidence of the birth or death to which it relates without any further or other proof of the entry, and no certified copy purporting to have been given in the said Office shall be of any force or effect unless it is sealed or stamped as aforesaid.

CAUTION:—It is an offence to falsify a certificate or to make or knowingly use a false certificate or a copy of a false certificate intending it to be accepted as genuine to the prejudice of any person, or to possess a certificate knowing it to be false without lawful authority.

DX 324092

Form A504M Dd 8349771 20M 6/84 Mcr(304689)

46

I. JESSON OF HALIFAX, YORKSHIRE (continued)

This is the last Will and Testament of me William Jesson of Halifax in the County of York late Supervisor of Excise which I do make and publish as follows In the first place I direct all my just debts funeral and testamentary expenses to be paid by my Executors herein after named I give and bequeath unto my daughters Mary Ann the wife of William Hirst, Frances Jane, Emma and my Son William and my housekeeper Grace Lodge All the principal sum interest and Bonus that may due at my decease upon my Life Policy in equal shares Subject nevertheless to the payment of my said debts and funeral expenses and the proportion so given to my said housekeeper shall be taken and accepted by her as and in discharge of all accounts that may be due to her from me for her salary or otherwise All the household goods furniture and effects in and about my dwellinghouse and all other my personal estate and effects whatsoever and wheresoever I give and bequeath to my said Son William absolutely I appoint my son in law the said William Hirst Executor and my daughter Frances Jane Executrix of this my Will In Witness whereof I have hereunto set my hand this twentieth day of February 1857 . William Jesson . Signed by the said Testator as and for his last Will and Testament in the presence of us present at the same time who in his presence at his request and in the presence of each other have hereunto subscribed our names as witnesses . Mary Jessop . Thos. Jessop

3 folios

In Her Majesty's Court of Probate. Wakefield District Registry. On the 2nd day of June 1864 the Will of William Jesson late of Halifax in the County of York Superannuated Officer of Excise deceased was proved by the oaths of William Hirst and Frances Jane Jesson Spinster the daughter of the said deceased the Executors named in the said will they having been first sworn duly to administer Effects under £300. Probate extracted by The Executors.

I. JESSON OF HALIFAX, YORKSHIRE (continued)

PUBLIC RECORD OFFICE

Reference:—

R.G. 9 / 3283

COPYRIGHT PHOTOGRAPH—NOT TO BE REPRODUCED PHOTOGRAPHIC-ALLY WITHOUT PERMISSION OF THE PUBLIC RECORD OFFICE, LONDON

J. ADAMS OF OTHAM, KENT

CERTIFIED COPY OF AN ENTRY OF BIRTH

GIVEN AT THE GENERAL REGISTER OFFICE, LONDON

Application Number B61953

REGISTRATION DISTRICT Westminster

BIRTH in the Sub-district of St John Westminster in the County of Middlesex

Columns:—	1	2	3	4	5	6	7	8	9	10*
No.	When and where born	Name, if any	Sex	Name and surname of father	Name, surname and maiden surname of mother	Occupation of father	Signature, description and residence of informant	When registered	Signature of registrar	Name entered after registration
135	Sunday second August 1866 2 Marsham Street West.	Percy Roy	Boy	George Roy Adams.	Louisa Kate Adams formerly Wilmer.	Singer	E.R. Adams father 2 Marsham Street Westminster	Seventh Sept 1866	W.E.G. Pearce Registrar	/

CERTIFIED to be a true copy of an entry in the certified copy of a Register of Births in the District above mentioned.
Given at the GENERAL REGISTER OFFICE, LONDON, under the Seal of the said Office, the 12th day of September 19 85

BXB 101368

This certificate is issued in pursuance of the Births and Deaths Registration Act 1953. Section 34 provides that any certified copy of an entry purporting to be sealed or stamped with the seal of the General Register Office shall be received as evidence of the birth or death to which it relates without any further or other proof of the entry, and no certified copy purporting to have been given in the said Office shall be of any force or effect unless it is sealed or stamped as aforesaid.

CAUTION:—It is an offence to falsify a certificate or to make or knowingly use a false certificate or a copy of a false certificate intending it to be accepted as genuine to the prejudice of any person or to possess a certificate knowing it to be false without lawful authority.

*See note overleaf

Form A502M   Dd 8349844   100M   4/85   Mcr (306230)

49

J. ADAMS OF OTHAM, KENT (continued)

1871 Census Returns for Westminster

Residence	Name	Relationship to head	Status	Age	Rank/ Occupation	County of Origin	Where Born
28 Marsham St	George Adams	Head	M	45	Draper	Kent	Otham
	Louisa Adams	Wife	M	42		Bucks	Loughton
	Percy M Adams	son	U	4		28 Marsham Street	
	Ann Wilmer	m-in-law	widow	80	Annuitant	Bucks	North Crawley
	Alfred Newdeck	Assistant	U	20	Assistant	Norfolk	Broomshill
	John Capon	Apprentice	U	16	Apprentice	Suffolk	Teamlingham
	Sophia E Porter	Assistant	U	23	Assistant	Bucks	Burton Hartsho.
	Mary Vine	Assistant	U	20	Assistant	Middlesex	Pimlico
	Mary Millard	Servant	U	20	Servant	Bedfordshire	Aspley Guise

J. ADAMS OF OTHAM, KENT (continued)

Otham, Kent, Bishop's Transcripts. (All entries for ADAMS or variants.)

Christenings and Burials 1745–1862

30	Sep	1748	Richard Adams and Elisabeth Boreman botp married by banns
16	Feb	1750	Mary d.o. Richard and Elisabeth Adams, bpt
7	Oct	1753	Martha d.o. Richard and Elisabeth Adams, bpt
19	Jan	1755	Richard s.o. Richard and Elisabeth Adams, bpt
9	May	1756	Margaret d.o. Richard and Elisabeth Adams, bpt
9	Apr	1758	Sarah d.o. Richard and Elisabeth Adams, bpt
28	Oct	1759	Anne d.o. Richard and Elisabeth Adams, bpt
6	Dec	1761	Lucy d.o. Richard and Elisabeth Adams, bpt
19	Feb	1764	Priscilla d.o. Richard and Elisabeth Adams, bpt
25	Apr	1764	Priscilla Adams, an infant, buried
23	May	1766	Elizabeth wife of Richard Adams, buried
18	Oct	1768	John Adams bachelor and Elizabeth Raynolds spinster botp married by banns
3	Oct	1772	George Betts and Mary Adams botp married by licence
5	Nov	1776	James Betts otp bachelor and Martha Adams otp spinster married by banns
14	Jan	1777	Alexander Anderson otp bachelor and Margaret Adams of Bersted married by licence with consent of her parents
2	Nov	1781	Richard Adams of the parish of Leeds and Elizabeth White married by banns
1	May	1782	William Dawson of the parish of Detling and Sarah Adams otp married by banns
28	Aug	1782	John s.o. Richard and Elizabeth Adams, bpt
4	Oct	1784	Ann d.o. Richard and Elizabeth Adams, bpt
21	Feb	1787	Mary d.o. Richard and Elizabeth Adams, bpt
13	Aug	1790	Elizabeth d.o. Richard and Elizabeth Adams, bpt
27	May	1793	R Adams, buried
25	Aug	1806	Richard Adams yeoman from Leeds, buried
27	Jul	1807	John Adams and Jane Millgate botp married by licence
18	Jun	1808	Richard s.o. John and Jane Adams, bpt
29	Nov	1811	Catherine Alexander d.o. John and Jane Adams, bpt
28	Nov	1813	Jane d.o. John and Jane Adams of Otham, farmer, bpt
3	May	1816	John s.o. John and Jane Adams of Otham, farmer, bpt
25	Apr	1819	Mary d.o. John and Jane Adams of Otham, labourer, bpt
31	Mar	1822	Elizabeth d.o. John and Jane Adams of Otham, farmer, bpt
25	Jul	1825	George s.o. John and Jane Adams of Otham, farmer, bpt
19	Jul	1825	Elizabeth Adams aged 66 buried
27	Jul	1851	Alice d.o. John and Elizabeth Adams of 20 Fore Street, Cripplegate, London, draper, bpt
27	Jun	1852	Frank s.o. John and Elizabeth Adams of St. Giles, Cripplegate, London, draper, bpt
26	Dec	1859	John Adams of Otham aged 78 buried
24	Mar	1862	Jane Adams of Otham aged 80 buried

SECTION 4. ANSWERS TO SECTION 1

SET A	SET B	SET C	SET D
1. b	1. a	1. b	1. a
2. c	2. c	2. a	2. b
3. c	3. c	3. b	3. c
4. a	4. b	4. a	4. a
5. a	5. c	5. c	5. b
6. b	6. c	6. a	6. c
7. a	7. a	7. b	7. c
8. c	8. a	8. a	8. b
9. c	9. c	9. c	9. c
10. b	10. b	10. b	10. a

SET E	SET F	SET G
1. c	1. b	1. c
2. b	2. c	2. b
3. c	3. c	3. b
4. a	4. b	4. c
5. b	5. a	5. c
6. c	6. b	6. a
7. b	7. c	7. b
8. b	8. b	8. a
9. a	9. c	9. a
10. a	10. a	10. c

SECTION 4. ANSWERS TO SECTION 2

SET A

1. Helen Jones, late Wilson, formerly Higgins.

2. Relationship to head of household, birthplace, exact age.

3. Date and place of birth, given names, surname, sex of child, name and occupation of father, name and former surnames of mother, date of registration and name, description and residence of informant, any other names added after registration.

4. (a) Unmarried; (b) journeyman; (c) agricultural labourer; (d) female servant; (e) framework knitter.

5. Deaths in 1887, as now, had to be registered within 5 days. Either of these two dates may have been incorrectly copied or the statutory time limit had expired.

SET B

1. All are women. (a) One appointed to carry out the terms of a will; (b) one making a will; (c) a widow of a named person.

2. The infant was baptised in a private ceremony, possibly at the birth because it was not expected to survive. Later the infant underwent a separate ceremony at the church. This is recorded in the parish register as 'received into the church'.

3. Bishop's Transcripts, annually at Easter to the local bishop (or archdeacon in some dioceses).

4. The date of the marriage, names, abode and marital status of bride and groom; whether they could sign the register; whether the marriage was by licence or after calling of banns; whether the bride and groom were over 21 and names of officiating minister and witnesses.

5. Andrew, William, Joan/Joanna, James, Wilfred; Christopher, James, William, Thomas, John/Jonathan.

SET C

1. (a) Principal Probate Registry; (b) codicil; (c) letters of administration; (d) inventory; (e) executor/executrix; (f) Prerogative Court of Canterbury.

2. Married women, lunatics, prisoners, traitors or apostates and heretics, boys under 14 and girls under 12, slaves and idiots.

3. Name and marital status and description of the deceased, usual residence, place of death, date of death, names of executor(s) or administrator(s), their address(es), occupations and relationship(s) (if any) to the deceased; value of the estate, date of probate and the district probate registry which dealt with the estate.

4. (a) Prerogative Court of York or Prerogative Court of Canterbury; (b) Prerogative Court of Canterbury; (c) Prerogative Court of Canterbury.

5. A list of a deceased person's possessions, with their values. They were usually compiled by two disinterested local people. Likely to be found with the appropriate will for the period 1540 to 1782.

SET D

1. Details of Quaker persecutions.

2. (a) Both of this parish; (b) decessit sine prole (died without issue); (c) unmarried; (d) obiit/obierunt (he/they died).

3. Consult telephone directories which can be found in most libraries and large post offices. Write to relevant address, or place advertisement in local newspaper of area, where relative assumed to live.

4. National Genealogical Directory, Genealogical Research Directory, Guild Of One-Name Studies Register, Latter-Day Saints Family Registry, Family History Societies' members' interest lists, County Families series.

5. (a) National Genealogical Directory; (b) Genealogical Research Directory; (c) Latter-Day Saints; (d) Guild of One-Name Studies; (e) Federation of Family History Societies; (f) Society of Genealogists; (g) Institute of Heraldic and Genealogical Studies.

SET E

1. Office of Population Censuses and Surveys.

2. Birth, marriage or death certificate.

3. A multiple birth (e.g. twins or triplets etc).

4. An abstract is a summary of the salient points. A transcript is a word for word copy.

5. Boyd's Marriage Index, The International Genealogical Index, Pallot's Marriage Index, local marriage index for that county or area.

SET E

1. Birth, renting a property valued at more than £10 per annum, paying parish rates, serving as a parish official, completing a full term of apprenticeship, working in the parish under contract for a year and a day, marriage (for a woman).

2. Licence, bond, allegation.

3. The Trade section of a directory is an alphabetical listing of those who have paid to have their entry inserted indexed separately by the occupation that they pursue. The Commercial listing is an alphabetical sequence of all subscribers irrespective of their trade or occupation. The Court section is a further alphabetical listing usually of those of independent means, clergy, landed gentry and those who might be termed professionals.

4.

Snodland	John Molineaux	35	Ag Lab	I
or	Maria Molineaux	35		F
Burke Street	Philip Molineaux	15	Ag Lab	No
	Sarah Molineaux	12		Yes

5. Birthday book, memorial card, army discharge papers, school report, school prize, baptismal/confirmation certificate, family bible, diary and letters, etc.

SECTION 4. ANSWERS TO SECTION 3

A. BEECROFT

Beecroft of Bleasby, Nottinghamshire

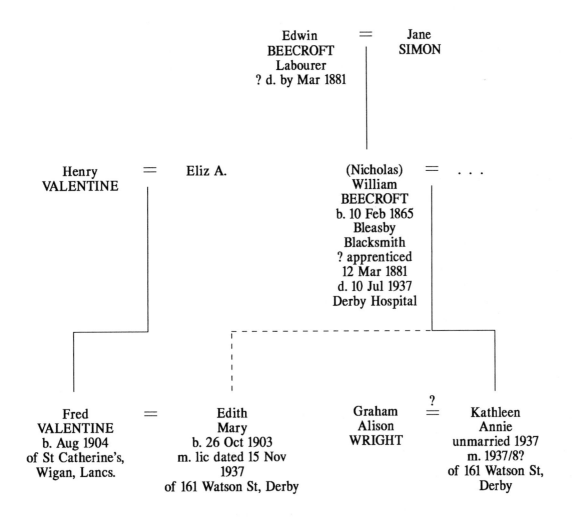

A. BEECROFT (continued)

This is intended as an introductory exercise to demonstrate how documents in family possession can provide the basic skeleton of a family tree and provide starting points for further research.

(NICHOLAS) WILLIAM

Birth and parentage come from Document A. Document B gives both his date of death and occupation as blacksmith and the initials of his daughter. Presumably this is KATHLEEN ANNIE who was unmarried in 1937. William was apprenticed to a blacksmith, THOMAS HASLAM of Lowdham, Nottinghamshire, in 1881 (Document F). He would appear to be unconnected with the family in Derby. However, NICHOLAS WILLIAM was born in Bleasby, and, although Bartholomew's Gazetteer includes two entries for Bleasby, an atlas will show that one of these is in the same part of Nottinghamshire as Lowdham. The mother of WILLIAM, who signed the indenture, was a widow named JANE, and NICHOLAS WILLIAM's mother was also JANE, according to his birth certificate. The term of the indenture ran from 10 February 1881 which would have been NICHOLAS WILLIAM BEECROFT's sixteenth birthday. It seems possible that WILLIAM BEECROFT who signed the indenture was NICHOLAS WILLIAM, and that his father, EDWIN, had died before March 1881.

EDITH MARY

The EDITH MARY born on 26 October 1903 (Document C) may be a daughter of NICHOLAS WILLIAM BEECROFT, but could be another relation. The licence for her marriage to FRED VALENTINE (Document D) was issued four months after NICHOLAS WILLIAM BEECROFT's death, and Document E gives some information about her husband. Document G is the piece of research on the family - an extract from the electoral register for Derby. This confirms that EDITH MARY was connected to NICHOLAS WILLIAM and KATHLEEN ANNIE BEECROFT, at least by residence, and also suggests that KATHLEEN ANNIE may have been married to GRAHAM ALISON WRIGHT about 1937/8.

KATHLEEN ANNIE

She was residing with NICHOLAS WILLIAM and EDITH MARY BEECROFT in 1936. After his death and the marriage of EDITH MARY in 1937, a KATHLEEN was found living with GRAHAM ALISON WRIGHT to whom she may well be married.

EDWIN

He is shown to be the father of NICHOLAS WILLIAM on the National Health Insurance Acts form of the birth certificate for 1865. On the apprenticeship indenture of 1881, JANE is shown to be a widow.

To confirm and extend the pedigree:

1. Obtain the full birth certificate of EDITH MARY BEECROFT, from St Catherine's House. As she was born on 26 October 1903, the entry should be found in the birth indexes for the December quarter of that year. The certificate should show her parentage. If she was NICHOLAS WILLIAM's daughter, this would provide the name of his wife.

2. A search should be made of the General Register Office indexes at St Catherine's House for a marriage of KATHLEEN ANNIE BEECROFT to GRAHAM ALISON WRIGHT in 1937 or 1938. The absence of such a marriage does not exclude the possibility that she adopted his name but a search of the indexes to the present day for her death, under both names, could provide an answer.

3. The 1881 census of Lowdham, Nottinghamshire, (at the Public Record Office, Chancery Lane) should be checked for a WILLIAM BEECROFT living with THOMAS HASLAM, a blacksmith. If WILLIAM's birthplace is given as Bleasby then the hypothesis that WILLIAM and NICHOLAS WILLIAM are one and the same person would be confirmed.

4. The General Register Office indexes should also be searched for the death of EDWIN BEECROFT prior to the June quarter of 1881 and for his marriage to JANE SIMON, probably prior to 1866.

5. A search should be made of the Principal Probate Registry, at Somerset House, for the will of EDWIN BEECROFT between 1865 and 1881.

B. STEVENS

Stevens of Bratton, Wiltshire

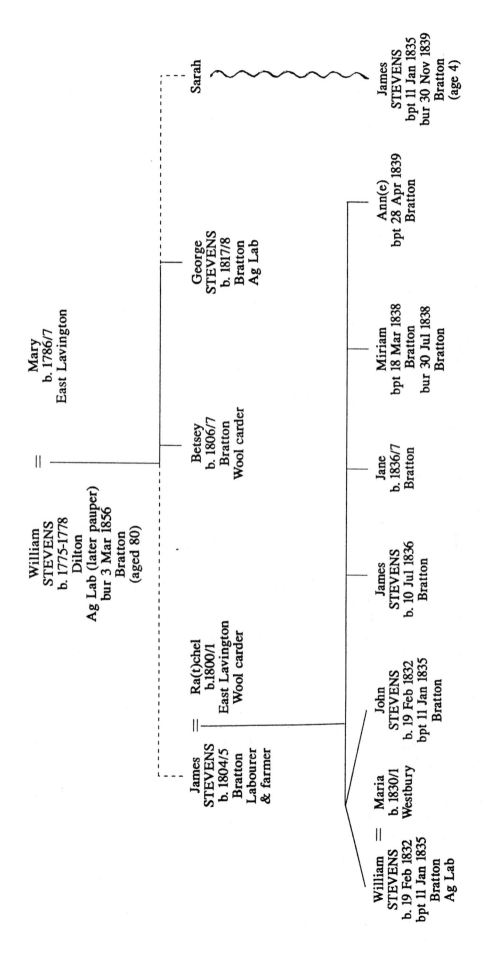

B. STEVENS (continued)

WILLIAM

The WILLIAM who is shown aged 73 in the census (born c. 1777/8) is almost certainly the same as WILLIAM given as aged 80 when buried in 1856 (born c. 1775/6). He and JAMES (born c. 1804/5) both found wives from East Lavington. WILLIAM could be the father of JAMES - and further research should confirm or deny this possibility. JAMES's eldest son (one of twins) was named WILLIAM - which could be evidence of a paternal grandfather naming pattern for the first male child.

JAMES

JAMES (born in 1804/5) rose in status from a labourer (until 1839) to a farmer of 20 acres by 1851.

SARAH

The mother of illegitimate JAMES could be the sister of JAMES (the farmer), since her child was baptised on the same day as JAMES's twins.

MIRIAM and ANNE

Their baptisms gave no mother's name but from other information it is clear that their mother was RACHEL.

To confirm and extend the pedigree:

1. Check the original parish registers for Bratton for the specific baptisms and burials given in the bishop's transcripts. Parish register and bishop's transcripts are frequently at variance; one may give more, or different, information from the other. Search all parish register entries of baptism, burial and marriage (1829–1859) for additional entries and in case any relevant entries have been omitted from the bishop's transcripts.

    Check earlier parish registers and bishop's transcripts for Bratton pre-1829. They may reveal, for example, the marriage of WILLIAM STEVENS and MARY, the baptisms of their children, the burials of members of earlier generations, and so on.

    The parish register and bishop's transcripts for Westbury, Dilton and East Lavington should be examined. In this way it may be possible to discover the marriages of WILLIAM STEVENS and MARY (1800–1805), of JAMES STEVENS and RACHEL (1820–1835), and of WILLIAM and MARIA (1847–1851). Refer to the Gibson Guide *Bishops' Transcripts and Marriage Licences: A Guide to their Location and Indexes* and to *The Phillimore Atlas and Index of Parish Registers* for the location of these records.

2. Examine later census returns for Bratton. These can be found at the Public Record Office, Chancery Lane or locally (refer to the Gibson Guide *Census Returns on Microfilm 1841–1881: A Directory to Local Holdings in Great Britain, Channel Islands, Isle of Man*). This should reveal other information and suggest when members of the family died or moved away.

3. Check for any relevant wills or administrations, both for the STEVENS family and for distaff families once these surnames are known. Such indexes will be available at the Wiltshire Record Office or the Public Record Office, Chancery Lane, for the period before 1858 and at the Principal Probate Registry (PPR) if the probate was granted from 1858 onwards.

4. Search the International Genealogical Index (IGI) for Wiltshire for STEVENS and variants to confirm and extend the pedigree. This can be consulted at Latter-Day Saints (LDS) Family History Centres, the Society of Genealogists (SOG), Institute of Heraldic and Genealogical Studies (IHGS) and some County Record Offices and large libraries. Check *The Phillimore Atlas and Index of Parish Registers* or the *Parish and Vital Records List* to see if this and neighbouring parishes are included in the IGI. As the IGI is a finding index, any relevant entries found should be checked against the original source.

C. KNIGHT

KNIGHT of London and Kent

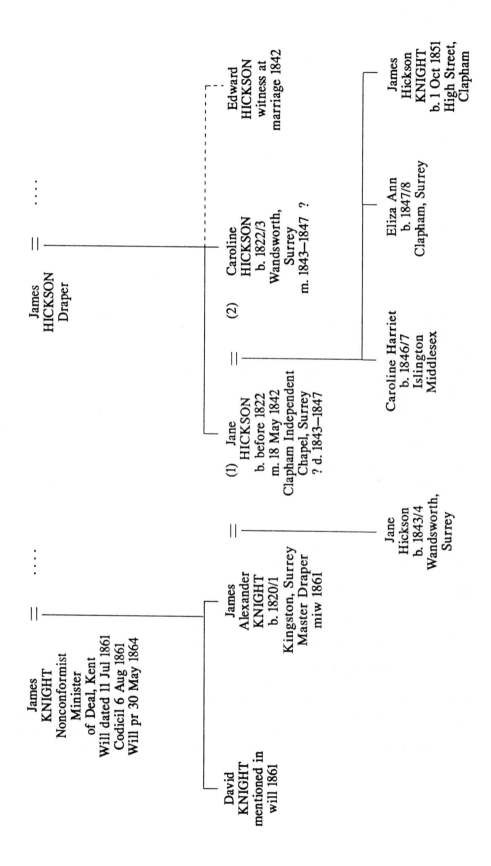

C. KNIGHT (continued)

JAMES
His will and the marriage certificate of his son JAMES ALEXANDER give his abode and occupation (note that he is the officiating minster at his son's marriage).

DAVID
He is mentioned in his father's will.

JAMES ALEXANDER
His father's name can be obtained from the will and the marriage certificate. His approximate year of birth and birth place are taken from the census extract which can be identified as that of 1851 from the call number and the information that it contains.

JAMES HICKSON
His name and occupation appear on the marriage certificate of his daughter, JANE.

JANE HICKSON
Her father's name is given on her marriage certificate which also implies that she was born prior to 1822. Her death is likely to have occurred between the birth of her daughter JANE and the birth of CAROLINE (HARRIET) KNIGHT, apparently a child of CAROLINE. This indicates that she was either divorced or deceased; at this date more probably the latter.

CAROLINE HICKSON
Her place and approximate year of birth are taken from the census extract. She was the younger sister of JANE HICKSON. Such a marriage to a deceased wife's sister did not become legal until 1907.

EDWARD HICKSON
He is a witness to JANE HICKSON's marriage. As he is not her father he is likely to be her brother.

JANE HICKSON
She appears in the census return described as 'former wife's daughter'. It is known from the marriage certificate that JAMES ALEXANDER KNIGHT was married to JANE HICKSON in 1842.

CAROLINE Ht (HARRIET?)
Described in the census returns as wife's daughter. This implies that she was the offspring of JAMES ALEXANDER and CAROLINE, as opposed to his 'former' wife.

JAMES HICKSON
His birth certificate gives the names of both his parents.

ELIZA ANN
She is shown as a daughter of JAMES ALEXANDER KNIGHT on the census return. There is no clear indication of who her mother was, but it is probably CAROLINE.

To confirm and extend the pedigree:

1. Obtain the birth certificates of JANE HICKSON KNIGHT (1843/4), CAROLINE (HARRIET) KNIGHT (1846/7) and ELIZA ANN KNIGHT (1847/8) to discover their exact dates of birth and their parentage. These certificates could be obtained from the General Register Office (St Catherine's House), or as the areas of birth are known, from the local register offices. An address list of local register offices (District Register Offices in England and Wales) has been published by East Yorkshire Family History Society.

2. The death indexes at the General Register Office (St Catherine's House) should be consulted for the death of JANE KNIGHT née HICKSON. The indexes from 1843 to 1847 should be checked. A search could then be conducted for the subsequent marriage of JAMES ALEXANDER KNIGHT to CAROLINE HICKSON. This would confirm the name of the bride's father. It may be that no such marriage took place due to the constraints of the law at that date.

3. Examine the International Genealogical Index (IGI) at Latter-Day Saints Family History Libraries or in other libraries. London, Surrey and Kent sections should be checked for the baptisms of DAVID and JAMES ALEXANDER KNIGHT, sons of JAMES. These baptisms are likely to have occurred in a nonconformist chapel between 1800 and 1840. The Surrey and London sections of the IGI should be checked for HICKSON and variants especially for the baptisms of JANE (born pre-1822), CAROLINE

c. 1823 and EDWARD in order to obtain exact dates, mother's christian name and the relationship of EDWARD to the two girls. The baptisms of JANE (c. 1844) and CAROLINE (c. 1847) may also be found under KNIGHT. *The Phillimore Atlas and Index of Parish Registers* or *The Parish and Vital Records List* should be used to discover if the IGI covers the likely parishes and nonconformists chapels. As the IGI is only a finding aid all information would need to be checked in the original registers.

4. Search nonconformist baptism records for Kingston, Surrey, for the baptism of JAMES ALEXANDER KNIGHT c. 1821 to obtain his date of baptism and the name of his mother. The baptism of DAVID and other children may also be found. Nonconformist baptisms often also include the maiden name of the mother. These records, as they pre-date 1837, should be at the Public Record Office in Chancery Lane (class RG4).

5. As he would have married between 1754 and 1837, probably at the end of the 18th or beginning of the 19th century, and as the terms of Lord Hardwicke's Marriage Act would be in operation, JAMES KNIGHT would have had to marry in the Church of England. His marriage could therefore be sought in the parish registers for Kingston, Surrey, prior to 1821. *The Phillimore Atlas and Index of Parish Registers* will show the whereabouts of the registers. If they are still with the incumbent his address will need to be obtained from *Crockford's Clerical Directory* which can be seen in reference libraries.

6. As he was a nonconformist minster, there may be biographical information concerning JAMES KNIGHT at the Dr. Williams's, Library, Gordon Square, London. This often provides a full life history as well as a date and place of birth.

7. Wills of other members of the KNIGHT family could be sought at the Principal Probate Registry (Somerset House) for the period from 1858. In particular the will of JAMES ALEXANDER KNIGHT could be useful. Pre 1858 wills might be found with records of Prerogative Court of Canterbury at the Public Record Office, Chancery Lane. *The Phillimore Atlas and Index of Parish Registers* and the Gibson Guide to *Probate Jurisdictions: Where to Look for Wills*, should be consulted to determine which other courts had jurisdiction in the appropriate areas and their records should also be checked for the wills of possible relevance. If the estate were of sufficient value to attract tax then the Death Duty Registers (IR 27) at the Public Record Office, Chancery Lane, could be used as a finding aid.

D. PARSLER

Parsler of Tetsworth, Oxfordshire

(All events took place in Tetsworth unless stated otherwise)

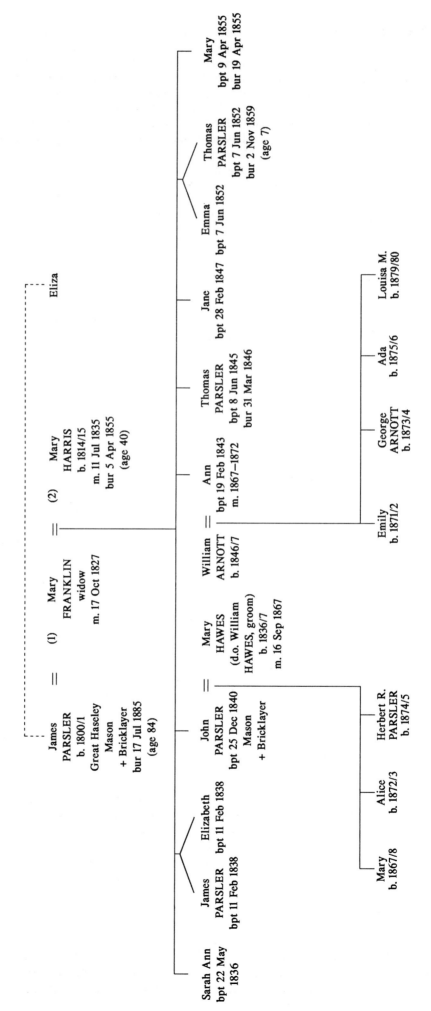

D. PARSLER (continued)

JAMES

He is recorded in the 1881 census returns of Tetsworth living with his son-in-law, WILLIAM ARNOTT, his daughter, ANN and the grandchildren. The age given to the census enumerator suggests a year of birth of 1800/1 and that he originated in Great Haseley. He was buried in Tetsworth in 1885 and the age again confirms a birth at the beginning of the 19th century. It is probable that JAMES and MARY (née HARRIS) had two sets of twins among their ten children. These are shown on the pedigree with the appropriate sign.

MARY FRANKLIN/MARY HARRIS

JAMES married twice according to the parish registers of Tetsworth. He was stated to be a widower when he married for the second time in 1835. Surprisingly the burial of his first wife is not recorded in the parish records. His second wife was buried in 1855, aged 40, under the spelling variant of PARSLOW.

ELIZA

Possibly a sister of JAMES as she was a witness at the marriage in 1827.

JOHN

He was baptised in Tetsworth on Christmas Day in 1840. His nine brothers and sisters were also christened there. The surname is occasionally recorded as PARSLOW. The father is stated to be a bricklayer, a mason or a labourer. In 1867 when JOHN married he described his father as a mason. JOHN and his wife MARY were recorded in the 1881 census with their children.

ANN

The information about her husband and children is to be found in the 1881 census returns. If she was the ANN PARSLER who witnessed her brother's marriage in 1867 she must have married between 1867 and 1872.

To confirm and extended the pedigree:

1. It would be sensible to examine the parish registers of Great Haseley in Oxfordshire. It is possible that JAMES PARSLER or PARSLOW and his first wife MARY (previously married to Mr FRANKLIN) had other children baptised there between 1827 and the date of JAMES's second marriage in 1835. The entry for the burial of MARY might also be recorded in these records. This would provide her age at death.

2. The baptismal records of Great Haseley should also be searched for the christening of JAMES PARSLER or PARSLOW circa 1800/1. This will provide the names of his parents and their marriage could then be sought. Furthermore a search in the burial records of the parish might show their ages at death. Such information is usually recorded in parish registers after 1812 when the new printed books were introduced by George Rose's Act.

   The present location of the parish registers could be established by reference to *The Phillimore Atlas and Index of Parish Registers* or by contacting the Oxfordshire County Record Office. If the registers remain with the incumbent, an appointment could be made to view them in the parish or the bishop's transcripts could be used instead. These are likely to be in the appropriate Diocesan Record Office (refer to the Gibson Guide *Bishop's Transcripts and Marriage Licences: A Guide to their Location and Indexes*). Alternatively a modern transcript of the parish register may be available at the Society of Genealogists Library.

3. As the name PARSLER and its variant spellings is probably reasonably uncommon the occurrence of the surname in the 18th century could be localised using the local marriage index. *The Oxfordshire Marriage Index* is now available in the County Record Office. A listing of all references to grooms with the surname PARSLER etc. could be made from this useful finding aid. The names of the parishes provided will suggest which other parish registers would be worthy of further investigation. If the marriage of the parents of JAMES born 1800/1 is not found in Great Haseley, it could be identified using such an index. Marriages for his grandparents and great-grandparents may also be found in the same manner (refer to the Gibson Guide *Marriage, Census and Other Indexes for Family Historians*).

4. If the baptism of JAMES PARSLER is not found in the registers of Great Haseley this would suggest that he was mistaken about his place of birth, or that his son-in-law, who presumably provided the information to the enumerator, gave an erroneous locality, or JAMES was baptised elsewhere or was not baptised. It should be remembered that place of birth and place of baptism are not necessarily the same. JAMES's

D. PARSLER (continued)

parents may have been nonconformists and used a local chapel of another denomination. By consulting the International Genealogical Index (IGI) for Oxfordshire and the adjacent counties, a possible baptism (or birth entry) may be found for JAMES c. 1800/1. This would be a particularly sensible search if non conformity was suspected. The majority of nonconformist protestant registers collected in 1837 and 1840 and now available at the Public Record Office, Chancery Lane, have been filmed and included in the IGI. The IGI is available at Latter-Day Saints (LDS) Family History Centres, the Society of Genealogists (SOG), Institute of Heraldic and Genealogical Studies (IHGS) and some County Record Offices and large libraries. Once a possible baptism for JAMES has been located all efforts should be made to prove that this is not the man who married in 1827 before he can be accepted as the forebear of the PARSLER family of Tetsworth.

5. Although it might be expected that bricklayers and masons did not leave probate documents it would be worth consulting the calendars and indexes available for relevant ecclesiastical jurisdictions that had authority over the area of Great Haseley and Tetsworth (refer to Gibson Guide - Probate Jurisdictions: Where to look for wills). Such wills and administrations before 1858 will either be in the appropriate Diocesan Record Office or, if proved in the Prerogative Court of Canterbury, will be in the Public Record Office, Chancery Lane. From 1812 indexes to the so-called Inland Revenue wills and administrations (IR 27) would be quicker and more efficient than conducting searches in the indexes and calendars of all relevant probate courts. If the will or administration was proved or granted from 1858 the document would be found in The Principal Probate Registry, Somerset House. It is possible that such a document could be found for JAMES PARSLER who died in 1885.

E. BAYLIS

Baylis of Kempsey, Worcestershire

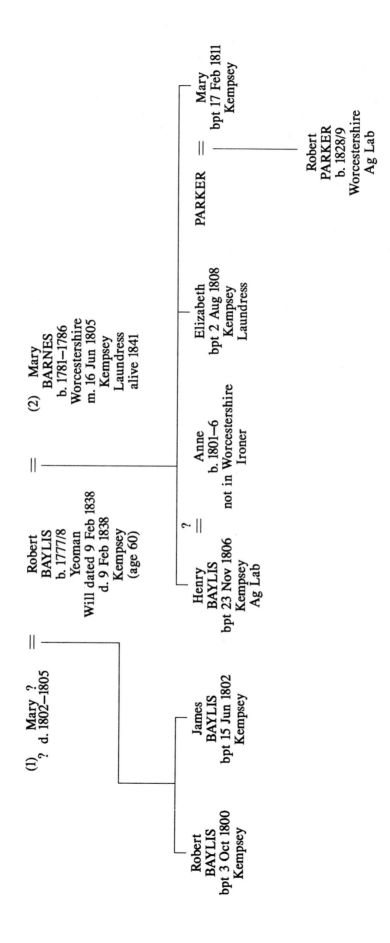

E. BAYLIS (continued)

ROBERT senior

His approximate year of birth is obtained from the age given on his death certificate. Note the different spelling of the surname in the text of the will (BAYLIS) and in ROBERT's signature (BAILIS).

MARY

It is possible that ROBERT had two wives called MARY. MARY BAYLI(E)S née BARNES is the only one about whom we have any information. Her year of birth can be estimated within five years from the census return which can be identified as that of 1841 because of its format. The marriage entry for ROBERT BAYLIS and MARY BARNES should have shown their marital status but this had been omitted from the parish register. Perhaps ROBERT and MARY married after the baptisms of their first two children.

ROBERT junior

It can be seen from his baptismal entry that he is the son of ROBERT and MARY. This may not be MARY BAYLIS née BARNES as there is no hint of illegitimacy in the baptismal entry. His status as ROBERT's son is confirmed by the will.

JAMES

His baptismal entry identifies him as son of ROBERT. The absence of a mother's name could suggest that his mother was dead by this time. Registers of this date usually (but not invariably) name both parents; the other baptismal entries show that this is the practice in Kempsey. He is also mentioned in the will.

HENRY

From his baptismal date he can be assumed to be the son of ROBERT and MARY BAYLIS née BARNES. Again the will confirms that he belongs to the family.

ANNE

The census return indicates, but does not prove, that she may be the wife of HENRY. She could be another daughter of ROBERT and MARY but this is unlikely as she was born in another county and is not mentioned in the will. She could, of course, be connected in some other way.

ELIZABETH

Her parents are given in her baptismal entry and her father is confirmed by the will.

MARY

Her parents are given in her baptismal entry. Her marriage to Mr. PARKER is revealed in the will.

ROBERT PARKER

He could be the son of MARY PARKER née BAYLIS but there is no proof as relationships are not shown in the 1841 census. He could also be a relative of MARY's husband Mr PARKER, such as a younger brother or nephew.

Transcript of the Will of ROBERT BAYLIS, Kempsey, Worcester, 1838

I ROBERT BAYLIS of Norman Common in the parish of Kempsey in the County of Worcester do make this my last Will and Testament I give & devise unto my Wife MARY BAYLIS all the little Property I am possessed of the Cottage built by me situate lying & being on the Border of Norman Common with the Garden adjoining, to have & to hold to her her heirs & assigns for Ever & also all the furniture in the said Cottage & all the Vegetables in the said Garden & all the money I may be possessd of at my decease, to be Enjoyed by her as long as She may live - If, however, She may not wish to sell the said Cottage & Garden to provide for her maintenance during her natural Life, It is my Will that the said Cottage & Garden be sold at her Decease & Equally divided between my five Children, ROBERT BAYLIS, JAMES BAYLIS, HENRY BAYLIS, ELIZABETH BAYLIS and MARY PARKER share & share alike & that all the Household Furniture be equally divided between my two Daughters ELIZABETH BAYLIS & MARY PARKER, & I appoint my said Wife MARY BAYLIS, Executrix of this my Will, In Witness Whereof I, the said Testator ROBERT BAYLIS have set my hand & seal this ninth Day of February 1838

signed ROBERT BAILES

Signed, sealed, published & declared in the presence of the Testator as & for his last Will & Testament, & in the Presence of us who in the presence of Each other have subscribed our names as Witnesses Matthew Lunn Vicar of Kempsey The Mark of Hester Etheridge

E. BAYLIS (continued)

To confirm and extend the pedigree:

1. Search the burial register for Kempsey, Worcestershire 1800–1805 for a burial of MARY BAYLIS (and variants) to confirm that MARY BARNES is a second wife. The Phillimore Atlas and Index of Parish Registers will show if the registers have been deposited. They will probably be at the Worcestershire Record Office (refer to the Gibson Guide *Record Offices: How to Find Them*). Alternatively the registers may be with the incumbent whose address can be found in *Crockford's Clerical Directory*, available in reference libraries. If so, the bishop's transcripts (refer to the Gibson Guide *Bishops' Transcripts and Marriage Licences: A Guide to their Location and Indexes*) could be used in the Diocesan Record Office. It is possible that ROBERT and MARY married after the births of their first two children. If so, no burial of Mary will be found in this record.

2. Examine the section of the International Genealogical Index (IGI) for Worcestershire and surrounding counties, including Wales, for a possible first marriage of ROBERT BAYLIS (and variants) to MARY .... between 1790 to 1800. The IGI can be consulted at LDS Family History Centres, the Society of Genealogists, Institute of Heraldic and Genealogical Studies and some County Record Offices and large libraries. Check *The Phillimore Atlas and Index of Parish Registers* or *The Parish and Vital Records List* to see which parishes are included in the IGI. Any entry found should be checked against the parish register. Alternatively the marriage bond and allegation could be consulted as the union in 1805 took place by licence. If these survive they will be in the Diocesan Record Office (refer to the Gibson Guide *Bishops' Transcripts and Marriage Licences: A Guide to their Location and Indexes*). This should confirm whether ROBERT was a widower or bachelor when he married MARY BARNES.

3. Search the 1851 census return for Kempsey, Worcestershire, hoping to discover the relationship of ANNE BAYLIS and/or ROBERT PARKER to the rest of the family. The census could be examined at the Public Record Office, Chancery Lane, or in a local repository (refer to the Gibson Guide *Census Returns on Microfilm 1841–1881: A Directory to Local Holdings in Great Britain, Channel Islands, Isle of Man*). The 1851 census returns may have been indexed by local family history societies.

4. Search the baptismal register of Kempsey, Worcestershire for the christening of ROBERT BAYLIS (and variants) 1770–1800 (this date span is necessary in case the age at death is inaccurate and because he may not have been baptised as an infant). *The Phillimore Atlas and Index of Parish Registers* will show if the registers have been deposited. They will probably be at the Hereford and Worcester Record Office (refer to the Gibson Guide *Record Offices: How to Find Them*). Alternatively the registers may be with the incumbent whose address can be found in *Crockford's Clerical Directory*, available in reference libraries. Again in the absence of the parish registers the bishop's transcripts may act as an alternative source of this information (refer to the Gibson Guide *Bishops' Transcripts and Marriage Licences: A Guide to their Location and Indexes*).

F. OUGH

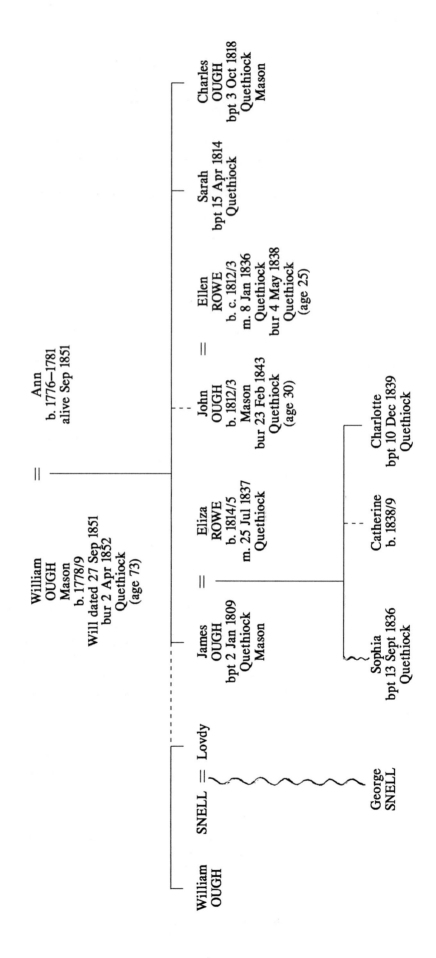

Ough of Quethiock, Cornwall

William OUGH

SNELL = Lovdy

George SNELL

William OUGH
Mason
b. 1778/9
Will dated 27 Sep 1851
bur 2 Apr 1852
Quethiock
(age 73)

= Ann
b. 1776–1781
alive Sep 1851

James OUGH
bpt 2 Jan 1809
Quethiock
Mason

= Eliza ROWE
b. 1814/5
m. 25 Jul 1837
Quethiock

John OUGH
b. 1812/3
Mason
bur 23 Feb 1843
Quethiock
(age 30)

= Ellen ROWE
b. c. 1812/3
m. 8 Jan 1836
Quethiock
bur 4 May 1838
Quethiock
(age 25)

Sarah
bpt 15 Apr 1814
Quethiock

Charles OUGH
bpt 3 Oct 1818
Quethiock
Mason

Sophia
bpt 13 Sept 1836
Quethiock

Catherine
b. 1838/9

Charlotte
bpt 10 Dec 1839
Quethiock

F. OUGH (continued)

WILLIAM senior
    His approximate year of birth is obtained from his age at burial.

ANN
    A very rough year of birth can be calculated from the census return.

LOVDY and WILLIAM
    The will shows that they are WILLIAM's children but there is no proof of who their mother was. It was not necessarily ANN as WILLIAM may have married more than once.

JAMES
    His baptism entry shows both parents. The name of his father is confirmed in JAMES's marriage entry.

ELIZA
    Her approximate year of birth can be obtained from her marriage entry.

SARAH and CHARLES, SOPHIA and CHARLOTTE
    Their baptismal entries showed the names of their parents.

JOHN
    Probably another child of WILLIAM and ANN. His age at burial gives a birth date between JAMES and SARAH, so if he is WILLIAM's son he is likely also to be Ann's. He is with them in 1841 but as no relationships are given he need not be a son (he could be a nephew for example). JOHN and ELLEN were witnesses at the marriage of JAMES and ELIZA and vice versa. This indicates a close relationship.

ELLEN
    Her approximate year of birth can be obtained from her age at burial.

GEORGE SNELL
    The will implies that LOVDY was still LOVDY OUGH in 1851 making GEORGE SNELL illegitimate (it is just possible that LOVDY married Mr. SNELL then remarried to Mr. OUGH). The evidence from the will is inconclusive she could have been LOVDY SNELL at this date.

CATHERINE
    Is almost certainly another child of JAMES and ELIZA.

Transcript of Will of WILLIAM OUGH, Quethiock, Cornwall, 1851

I WILLIAM OUGH of Quethiock in the County of Cornwall (Mason) do make my last Will and Testament in manner following. First I Give and bequeath unto my Four Children, JAMES, LOVDY, SARAH, and WILLIAM OUGH all the Public House, Garden, Stable Barn Chall and Pigs houses thereunto belonging to be equally shared among them. Secondly I Give and bequeath unto my son CHARLES OUGH all that Dwelling House and Pigshouse situated near to or adjoining the Public House, now in my own occupation, I Give unto JAMES my son my Hanging Press now in my Possession. I Give unto LOVDY my Daughter my Large Clothes Chest now in my Possession. I Give unto SARAH my daughter my small Table now in my possession. I Give unto WILLIAM my Son my Clock now in my possession. I Give unto CHARLES my Son my Bed and Bedding, now in my possession also my Chest of Drawers (and Grates (being in my possession, and I Give and bequeath unto all my Children (to be equally divided among them all my other Goods Chattels and effects whatsoever and wheresoever situated not being mentioned in this my Will, Also I Give unto ANN OUGH my Wife the sum of Eight Pounds Pr year solong as she shall live, to be paid Her Yearly or otherwise as she may require after my Decease from the Rents arising from the Property which I now bequeath unto my Children That is to say One Pound Twelve shillings to be paid Her Annually or otherwise as she may require from each of my Five Children, I also Give unto GEORGE SNELL son of my Daughter LOVDY the sum of Five Pounds to be paid Him at my Death out of the money that will be due to me from the Death Club at Liskeard. And lastly it is my Will that the Remainder of the money of the Liskeard Club together with that of Quethiock Club shall be equally divided among all my Children together with ANN OUGH my Wife, First deducting all reasonable expenses for my Funeral out of it and also for ANN OUGH my wife to have the management of my Funeral Expenses,

And I hereby nominate and appoint JAMES and WILLIAM OUGH my sons, Executors of this my last Will and Testament, Witness my Hand this Twenty Seventh day of September in the Year of Our Lord One Thousand Eight Hundred and Fifty One   WILLIAM OUGH

Signed by the said Testator in the presence of us who in his presence, and in the presence of each other have hereunto subscribed our names as Witnesses   Samuel Rogers Robert H. Greet

F. OUGH (continued)

To confirm and extend the pedigree:

1. Search for the birth certificate of CATHERINE OUGH. The certificate could be obtained from the Superintendent Registrar for the district which covers Quethiock. If this failed use the General Register Office indexes at St Catherine's House or on film or fiche at a local library (e.g. Latter-Day Saints (LDS) Family History Library, or Society of Genealogists (SOG)). Search in the indexes for 1838 and 1839. It might also be necessary to search a slightly wider date span in case her age was given incorrectly in the 1841 census to obtain a certificate from the General Register Office. It will be necessary to search under all variants of the surname. This should confirm whether she was the daughter of JAMES and ELIZA.

2. Examine the baptism register for Quethiock 1770–1800 for the christening of WILLIAM OUGH senior (and variants of the surname). It is necessary to search this time period in case the age at death is inaccurate or in case he was baptised as an adult. A baptismal entry at this time is likely to provide the christian names of both parents. *The Phillimore Atlas and Index of Parish Registers* will show if the registers have been deposited. This will probably be at the Cornwall Record Office (refer to the Gibson Guide *Record Offices: How to Find Them*). Alternatively the registers may be with the incumbent whose address can be found in *Crockford's Clerical Directory*, available in reference libraries. Bishop's transcripts may also survive for this period and will be in the Diocesan Record Office (refer to the Gibson Guide *Bishops' Transcripts and Marriage Licences: A Guide to their Location and Indexes*).

3. Search the marriage register of Quethiock 1792–1809 for the union of WILLIAM OUGH senior (or variants of surname) and ANN . . . . (this date span is necessary in case WILLIAM married at the minimum age of 14). Other relevant marriages may be found. This may confirm if WILLIAM had been married previously. The maiden name(s) of the bride(s) should thus be discovered with the names of relevant witnesses. Again the appropriate sources should be consulted to discover where the records or copies of them could be examined. If the marriage was performed by licence this would lead to other documents such as the marriage bond and allegation. *The Phillimore Atlas and Index of Parish Registers* will show if the registers have been deposited. These will probably be at the Cornwall Record Office (refer to the Gibson Guide *Record Offices: How to Find Them*). Alternatively the registers may be with the incumbent whose address can be found in *Crockford's Clerical Directory*, available in reference libraries. If the marriage is not found in the parish records of Quethiock, it might be located in another parish by using the International Genealogical Index (IGI) for Cornwall. This can be consulted at Latter-Day Saints (LDS) Family History Centres, the Society of Genealogists (SOG), Institute of Heraldic and Genealogical Studies (IHGS) and some County Record Offices and large libraries.

4. Search for entries for OUGH and variants in the 1851 census returns for Quethiock. These should show any subsequent children of JAMES and ELIZA and may also show a family for CHARLES thus extending the tree downwards. The census returns at the census Rooms at the Public Record Office, Chancery Lane, or in a local repository (refer to the Gibson Guide *Census Returns on Microfilm 1841–1881: A directory to local holdings in Great Britain, Channel Islands, Isle of Man*). Check to see if the census has been indexed, perhaps by the local family history society.

5. As WILLIAM OUGH left a will, it may be that probate material, wills and administrations, survive for other members of the family. A search should be conducted in the calendar of probate documents for the ecclesiastical jurisdictions which existed in Cornwall pre-1858. Wills may also have been proved in the Prerogative Court of Canterbury (PCC). These wills are at the Public Record Office, Chancery Lane (refer to the Gibson Guide *Probate Jurisdictions: Where to Look for Wills*). For the period after 1800 no index has yet been printed for this probate court.

G. BARROW

Barrow of Woolastone, Gloucestershire
(all events took place in Woolastone)

George BUCKLE = Mary

George BUCKLE b. 1685/6 d. 16 Nov 1773 (age 87) = Mary d. 12 Dec 1733 ?

Richard BARROW gent d. 23 Jun 1720 = Elizabeth bur 20 Mar 1757 ?

Walter HARRIS = Ann b. 1712/3 d. 20 Oct 1786 (age 73)

William HARRIS sailmaker b. 1733/4 d. 29 Jun 1799 (age 65)

Richard HARRIS tanner

John BARROW gent b. 1697/8 d. 12 Dec 1775 bur 14 Dec 1775 (age 77) = Elizabeth bur 20 Mar 1757 ?

John BARROW Will dated 7 Oct 1782 bur 5 Sep 1784 Will pr 9 Mar 1785

(1) Frances bur 30 Jun 1752 = ? = (2) Elizabeth bur 20 Mar 1757 ?

John BARROW bpt 12 Jun 1746 gent of Woolastone Grange = Love b. 1747/8 d. 18 May 1785 bur 11 May 1785 (age 37)

Richard BARROW bpt 14 Nov 1748 bur 3 May 1777 ? = Helen

John BARROW bpt 2 Jun 1773

Sarah bpt 12 Feb 1775

Another child

William WILLIAMS = Frances bpt 22 Nov 1744

John BARROW bpt 8 Jul 1743 bur 16 Aug 1743

John WILLIAMS

Henry WILLIAMS

Frances

Sarah

Mary

Richard WILLIAMS

John BARROW bpt 19 Mar 1777 bur 1 Apr 1777

John BARROW bpt 8 Jun 1778

Richard BARROW bur 1 Feb 1780

Elizabeth bpt 16 May 1780

Sarah bur 5 Nov 1781

Richard BARROW bpt 13 Oct 1782

James BARROW bpt 31 Jul 1785 bur 19 Mar 1787

G. BARROW (continued)

Some of the individuals recorded on the monumental inscription cannot be included on the pedigree.

RICHARD

His date of death is recorded on the monumental inscription.

ANN and MARY

From the information given on the monumental inscription it seems most likely that they were born close to the beginning of the 18th century. Indeed ANN's age suggests a year of birth of 1712/3. Both were stated to be daughters of RICHARD BARROW. ANN was also the wife of WALTER HARRIS and it is possible that WILLIAM and RICHARD HARRIS were her sons. WILLIAM was born c. 1733/4 according to his age at death.

MARY

Became the wife of GEORGE BUCKLE born c. 1685/6.

JOHN senior

Is probably a son of RICHARD BARROW (gent) who was mentioned on the memorial recorded in *Bigland's Gloucestershire Collections*. His year of birth calculated from his age at death is 1697/8.

JOHN junior

Left a will written in 1782 and proved in 1785. He is known to have been buried in 1784 at Woolastone when he is called 'JOHN BARROW senior', his father having died nine years earlier. It is possible that he was married twice, firstly to FRANCES, buried in 1752, and secondly to ELIZABETH, who died in 1757. It is also possible from the information available that Mrs ELIZABETH BARROW was the wife of JOHN BARROW senior.

FRANCES

Was married to WILLIAM WILLIAMS according to the bequest in the will of JOHN BARROW junior proved in 1785. She had six known children.

JOHN

Is stated to be of Woolastone Grange in the will of his father.

LOVE

Would have been born about 1747/8 according to her age at death. It is interesting to note that her date of death recorded on the monumental inscription is seven days *after* her burial!

RICHARD

Son of JOHN and FRANCES BARROW was baptised in 1748. Two of his children were recorded in the parish registers but in the will of JOHN, RICHARD is stated to have three children. It is possible that RICHARD was already dead by the time that JOHN wrote his will as there is a burial for a RICHARD on 3 May 1777. If so, it is surprising that he was not referred to as 'my late son RICHARD BARROW'.

RICHARD

An infant buried 1 February 1780. He may have been a further child of JOHN and LOVE BARROW whose baptism is not recorded in the parish registers.

To confirm and extend the pedigree:

1. The parish registers and bishop's transcripts for Woolastone post-1813 should be searched especially for burial entries. These are likely to be deposited in the Gloucestershire Record Office or may remain with the incumbent. Their locality can be ascertained by reference to *The Phillimore Atlas and Index of Parish Registers*. From 1813 ages of the deceased will be recorded in the burial register. Entries for JOHN of Woolastone Grange, his brother RICHARD and HELEN BARROW should be sought. These could confirm whether or not RICHARD BARROW was dead by 1782 when his father's will was written and if the entry for 1777 refers to the burial of this RICHARD.

2. It is necessary to locate several marriages which are missing from the pedigree. These did not take place in the parish church of Woolastone between 1740 and 1800, unless they have been missed by the transcriber. By consulting the International Genealogical Index for Gloucestershire, and the surrounding counties, the marriage entries for JOHN BARROW senior and junior may be found. In this way, it should be possible to determine if JOHN BARROW junior had married twice, his second marriage to ELIZABETH occurring between 1752 and 1757. Alternatively she may have been married to JOHN BARROW senior.

G. BARROW (continued)

The marriages of JOHN BARROW and LOVE and of RICHARD BARROW and HELEN may also be located. If the appropriate marriages are not located here they may be found in *Boyd's Marriage Index* for Gloucestershire (also called *Roe's Marriage Index*) available at the SOG or in some local record offices and libraries.

3. To extend the pedigree it would be necessary to consult the parish registers (or bishop's transcripts) of Woolastone. The baptismal, marriage and burial entries from 1660 to 1739 should be searched. This should confirm the information recorded on the monumental inscription and may locate the baptism of JOHN BARROW c. 1697/8 if he originated in Woolastone. The baptisms of MARY and ANN (born c. 1712/3) may also be found. It is likely that RICHARD BARROW and his wife will also be recorded in the burial registers pre-1740.

    If the family had lived in the parish for some time, as suggested by their landed status, then the baptism of RICHARD BARROW and his marriage may also have taken place in the parish church. If entries for these events are not located in the records of Woolastone then the IGI for Gloucestershire and the surrounding area should be examined.

4. As the family had property and estates, it is quite likely that other probate documents survive. The printed indexes to the Gloucestershire probate records and to the Prerogative Court of Canterbury (PCC), Chancery Lane, London should be searched for the period 1600 to 1800. Unfortunately the printed indexes to the PCC only cover the period to 1700 and from 1750 to 1800. Refer to the Gibson Guide *Probate Jurisdictions: Where to Look for Wills*. However from these it should be possible to locate any surviving will for JOHN BARROW senior who died in 1775 and for FRANCES (died 1752), ELIZABETH (died 1757) and LOVE who died in 1785.

The indexes for both courts before 1700 may reveal wills for people from earlier generations. It would be hoped that a will for RICHARD's father could be found in which he is specifically named. If the will of RICHARD BARROW (d. 1720) was not proved in Gloucestershire then a search of the original calendars of the PCC would have to be made for the period 1720 to 1725 to allow for the process of probate.

To locate any surviving will for JOHN BARROW the calendars of the relevant probate court would need to be examined. Alternatively the indexes to the Inland Revenue or Estate Duty wills, at the Public Record Office, Chancery Lane, could be searched from 1812 (IR 27). Using this source, it would not matter that the probate court which had proved the will was not known.

Any will for testators with the surname BARROW who lived in the Woolastone area should be read and the genealogical information extracted. It may also be worth reading wills which may be found for testators called BUCKLE and HARRIS!

H. MUFFET

Muffet of St Columb Minor, Cornwell

(All entries are recorded in parish registers of St Columb Minor)

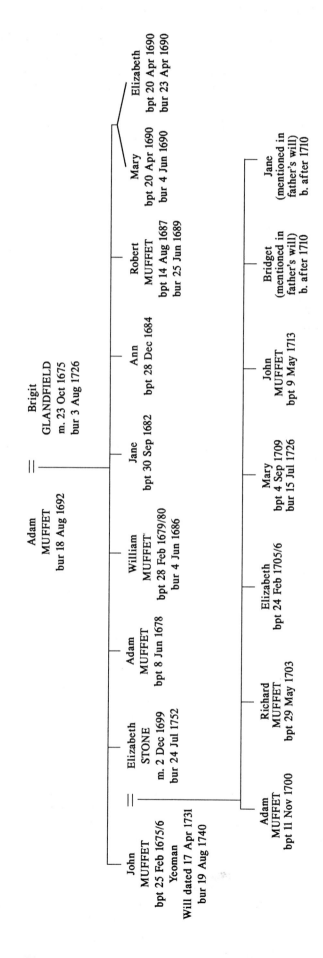

Adam
MUFFET
bur 18 Aug 1692

═══ Brigit
GLANDFIELD
m. 23 Oct 1675
bur 3 Aug 1726

John
MUFFET
bpt 25 Feb 1675/6
Yeoman
Will dated 17 Apr 1731
bur 19 Aug 1740

═══ Elizabeth
STONE
m. 2 Dec 1699
bur 24 Jul 1752

Adam
MUFFET
bpt 8 Jun 1678

William
MUFFET
bpt 28 Feb 1679/80
bur 4 Jun 1686

Jane
bpt 30 Sep 1682

Ann
bpt 28 Dec 1684

Robert
MUFFET
bpt 14 Aug 1687
bur 25 Jun 1689

Mary
bpt 20 Apr 1690
bur 4 Jun 1690

Elizabeth
bpt 20 Apr 1690
bur 23 Apr 1690

Adam
MUFFET
bpt 11 Nov 1700

Richard
MUFFET
bpt 29 May 1703

Elizabeth
bpt 24 Feb 1705/6

Mary
bpt 4 Sep 1709
bur 15 Jul 1726

John
MUFFET
bpt 9 May 1713

Bridget
(mentioned in
father's will)
b. after 1710

Jane
(mentioned in
father's will)
b. after 1710

H. MUFFET (continued)

Transcript of Will of John Muffet of St Columb Minor, 1731

In the name of god Amen I JOHN MUFFAT of the p(ar)ish of Collumbe minor in the County of Cornwall Yeoman beeing sick & wake but of good and perfect mind & memory thanks bee unto Allmighty God, And calling to mind the manyfeuld Sins And Transsgreasons of this transetorey Life I doe Recomend my Soul into the hands of Allmigty God and my Body to bee decently buryed According to the descreation of my Executrix in manor And form foweling

Imp(rimis) Itt I give unto my Son ADAM, on Feathar Bed furnshet

Itt I give uto my Son RICHARD my Land in Trenick to him and his heirs for Ever, to porssess the same at or within three years aftor my Deceas and the s^d RICHD MUFF to pay to his mother ELIZABETH MUFFT yearly out of the s^d Land the summe of Five pounds during her Natuerall life, and the Hall Chamber as a lodging During her life

Itt I do obledge my sd son RICHD to pay out of the Above sd Lands the sume of two hundred, pounds, two wards Depts and Leagacyes

Itt I give my wife the Bed furnshet over the halle and one brass Crock the midlemest two pater plates two plators and on Ocking Cheast

Itt I give my Daughter ELIZABETH the sume of fifty pounds to bee payd her at or within three years after my Deceas) on Bed furnsht and on hanging Press

Itt I give my Daughter BRIDGET the sume of Fiftey pounds to bee payd her at the Age of twenty on, but to Receive Intrest for the Same at or Imeadently, after my Deceas with a Bed furnsht

Itt I give my Daught(er) JANE fifty pounds to bee payd her at the Age of twenty one But to Receive Intrest for the same at or Imedently after my Deceas with a Beed Furnsht

Itt I give my Son JOHN on Chattle Estate in Nuckay now in my Porsseon the Lands of the Rig(ht) honarable Lord, Erle of Radnor and on Chattle Estat now In my Porssesion within the Vilege of Tenereck beeing the Lands of the Esqr Clabery

Itt I do herby constute And appoynt my well beloved wife to bee my holl and solle Executrix of this my last will and Teastement Revoking and Dissanouling all othar will or wills, of what Natuer or kind SoEver In witness wherof I here unto put my hand and seall this 17th Day of April Anoq Domini 1731

RICH^d PASCOE
WILL^m PERROE   JOHN MOFFATT

Memo^d If the s^d JOHN MUFFATs Effects do not hold out to pay the Depts and Leagecis then the Estate of Chatle in Newkay now the Lands of Mastor Pellamounto, is to bee sold, othar wayes I do setle the s^d Tenem^s on my sone JOHN by him To bee Enjoy^d during the live Thereon.

To confirm and extend the pedigree:

Although the name of the mother of the MUFFET children baptised at St Columb Minor between 1676 and 1690 is not recorded in the parish register, it can be assumed that all are children of BRIGIT since the couple married in 1675 and Brigit was buried in 1726. The last two children were twins and are indicated as such on the pedigree using the appropriate symbol.

Two additional children BRIDGET and JANE, were named by JOHN in his will. Both were stated to be under the age of 21 and must have been born after 1709. Either they were not christened or were baptised elsewhere.

1. Consult the parish registers of St Columb Minor for the period before 1675. The records of baptism, marriage and burial should be searched for any reference to Muffett and its variant spellings. It should be remembered that there is likely to be a gap in the parish registers and the bishop's transcripts from about 1640 to 1660 due to the Commonwealth Interregnum. It is probable that Adam was born in that period. By searching the period before 1640 it will be established if any people with the surname under investigation were using the church towards the beginning of the 17th century. They may represent an earlier generation. *The Phillimore Atlas and Index of Parish Registers* will show if the registers have been deposited. This will probably be at the Cornwall Record Office (refer to the Gibson Guide *Record Offices: How to Find Them*). Alternatively the registers may be with the incumbent whose address can be found in *Crockford's Clerical Directory*, available in reference libraries. Bishop's transcripts, if they survive, will be in the Diocesan Record Office (refer to the Gibson Guide *Bishops' Transcripts and Marriage Licences: A Guide to their Location and Indexes*).

H. MUFFET (continued)

2. Search the International Genealogical Index (IGI) for Cornwall. The IGI can be consulted at Latter-Day Saints (LDS) Family History Centres, the Society of Genealogists (SOG), Institute of Heraldic and Genealogical Studies (IHGS) and some County Record Offices and large libraries. Check *The Phillimore Atlas and Index of Parish Registers* or the *Parish and Vital Records List* to see which parishes are included in the IGI.

    If Cornwall is well covered by this index, this will allow the surname of Muffett and its variant spellings to be localised in parishes around St Columb Minor in the mid-seventeenth century. Any reference to ADAM MUFFET in the period before 1640 would be a possible clue to the earlier generations. The family used this christian name in three successive generations. The index may also produce the baptisms for BRIDGET and JANE MUFFET between 1710 and 1730 in a neighbouring parish or a nonconformist chapel.

3. The probate calendars and indexes for the ecclesiastical courts that had jurisdiction over this area of Cornwall should be consulted. *The Phillimore Atlas and Index of Parish Registers* or the Gibson Guide *Probate Jurisdictions: Where to Look for Wills* will indicate which probate courts had jurisdiction over St Columb Minor and the surrounding area and where the records are held. Locally these would be in the Diocesan Record Office. Wills may also have been proved in the Prerogative Court of Canterbury (PCC) and these are now at the Public Record Office, Chancery Lane. There are printed indexes for the period to 1700 and from 1750 to 1800 for this court.

    Any documents for testators who had the surname MUFFETT (or variant spellings) should be transcribed or abstracted. It may also be worth consulting the same source for testators called GLANDFIELD. The maternal grandfather of John Muffett baptised in 1676 is just as likely to leave a bequest to his grandson as is his paternal grandfather.

4. Mid-seventeenth century listings of inhabitants can be examined to determine the places where people with the surname Muffett lived. The Hearth Tax Returns of 1662–1689 will provide reference to where possible relatives lived after the Civil War (refer to the Gibson Guide *The Hearth Tax, Other Later Stuart Tax Lists and the Association Oath Rolls*). The Protestation Returns of 1641/2 will provide a similar localisation for the period at the beginning of the Interregnum or 'Commonwealth Gap'. By plotting such references on a parish map of Cornwall other parishes worthy of further investigation will be indicated. The original Hearth Tax Returns records are in the Public Record Office, Chancery Lane, and the Protestation Returns in The House of Lords Record Office. However there may be printed versions or facsimile copies available in the County Record Office.

I. JESSON

Jesson of Halifax, Yorkshire and Coston, Leicestershire

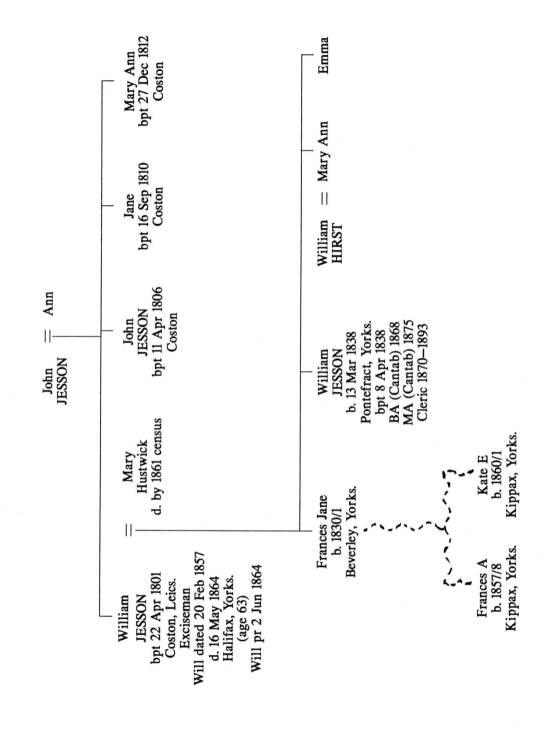

John
JESSON
= Ann

William
JESSON
bpt 22 Apr 1801
Coston, Leics.
Exciseman
Will dated 20 Feb 1857
d. 16 May 1864
Halifax, Yorks.
(age 63)
Will pr 2 Jun 1864

= Mary
Hustwick
d. by 1861 census

John
JESSON
bpt 11 Apr 1806
Coston

Jane
bpt 16 Sep 1810
Coston

Mary Ann
bpt 27 Dec 1812
Coston

Frances Jane
b. 1830/1
Beverley, Yorks.

William
JESSON
b. 13 Mar 1838
Pontefract, Yorks.
bpt 8 Apr 1838
BA (Cantab) 1868
MA (Cantab) 1875
Cleric 1870–1893

William
HIRST
= Mary Ann

Emma

Frances A
b. 1857/8
Kippax, Yorks.

Kate E
b. 1860/1
Kippax, Yorks.

I. JESSON (continued)

WILLIAM senior
Stated at his death to be an officer of the Inland Revenue. He died in 1864 in Halifax, aged 63, suggesting a year of birth of 1800/1. The informant was another WILLIAM JESSON, probably his son. The 1861 census entry for the same address is difficult to decipher but the birth place is shown to be in Leicestershire. Reference to *The Phillimore Atlas and Index of Parish Registers* suggests Coston as a likely interpretation of the place of birth recorded by the enumerator. The year of the baptism at Coston in 1801 agrees with the age given to the enumerator as does the age given on the death certificate. In his will he names a son WILLIAM.

FRANCES JANE
Is recorded as a daughter of WILLIAM JESSON senior in the 1861 census returns. The year of birth can be calculated from the age given to the enumerator.

WILLIAM junior
The entry in the Alumni of Cambridge University gives an exact date and place of birth and a date of baptism. It also provides the names of the parents. Most of the facts are confirmed by the birth certificate of WILLIAM. The continuity of the profession given for his father on the birth certificate, in the Alumni, in the will and on the death certificate of WILLIAM senior all provide confirmatory evidence that the two WILLIAMs are father and son.

EMMA and MARY ANN (wife of WILLIAM HIRST)
Described as daughters in the will of WILLIAM JESSON dated 1857.

FRANCES A and KATE E
Both born in Kippax, Yorkshire, and described in the census returns as the granddaughters of WILLIAM JESSON senior. They could be offspring of WILLIAM JESSON junior who was not at home on the night that the census was compiled. Alternatively they could be illegitimate daughters of FRANCES JANE the unmarried daughter of WILLIAM senior, who was at home on the night of the census.

Transcript of will of WILLIAM JESSON of Halifax, Yorkshire.

This is the last Will and Testament of me WILLIAM JESSON of Halifax in the County of York late Supervisor of Excise which I do make and publish as follows In the first place I direct all my just debts funeral and testamentary expenses to be paid by my Executors hereinafter named I give and bequeath unto my daughters MARY ANN the wife of WILLIAM HIRST, FRANCES JANE, origl so EMMA and my Son WILLIAM and my housekeeper GRACE LODGE All the principal sum interest and Bonus that may ... due at my decease upon my Life Policy in equal shares Subject nevertheless to the payment of my said debts and funeral expenses and the proportion so given to my said housekeeper shall be taken and accepted by her as and in discharge of all accounts that may be due to her from me for her salary or otherwise All the household goods furniture and effects in and about my dwellinghouse and all other my personal estate and effects whatsoever and wheresoever I give and bequeath to my said Son WILLIAM absolutely I appoint my son in law the said WILLIAM HIRST Executor and my daughter FRANCES JANE Executrix of this my Will In Witness whereof I have hereunto set my hand this twentieth day of February 1857 WILLIAM JESSON

Signed by the said Testator as and for his last Will and Testament in the presence of us present at the same time who in his presence at his request and in the presence of each other have hereunto subscribed our names as witnesses   MARY JESSOP   THOS. JESSOP

3 folios
In Her Majesty's Court of Probate Wakefield District Registry on the 2th day of June 1864 the Will of WILLIAM JESSON late of Halifax in the County of York Superannuated Officer of Excise deceased was proved by the oaths of WILLIAM HIRST and FRANCES JANE JESSON Spinster the daughter of the said deceased the Executors named in the said will they having been first sworn duly to adminster

Effects under £300
Probate extracted by
The Executors

I. JESSON (continued)

To confirm and extend the pedigree:

1. A search could be conducted in the 1851 census returns of 2 High Street, Halifax. If successful, this should reveal WILLIAM JESSON senior with his wife MARY and their offspring. The census material should include WILLIAM aged circa 13. If unsuccessful, the family might be found at 1 Horsefair, Pontefract. The census returns can be consulted at the Public Record Office, Chancery Lane, or in local record offices and libraries (refer to the Gibson Guide *Census Returns on Microfilm 1841–1881: A Directory to Local Holdings in Great Britain, Channel Islands, Isle of Man*).

2. The parish register of Beverley and Pontefract should be searched for baptisms for children of WILLIAM and MARY especially FRANCES JANE c. 1830/1, and WILLIAM on 8th April 1838. Other offspring should include MARY ANN and EMMA. The parish registers should be deposited in the appropriate County Record Office. Their present location can be determined by consulting *The Phillimore Atlas and Index of Parish Registers*. If the registers are not available, it should be possible to examine the appropriate bishop's transcripts. These will be in Diocesan Record Offices for the area (refer to the Gibson Guide *Bishops' Transcripts and Marriage Licences: A Guide to their Location and Indexes*).

3. The section of the International Genealogical Index (IGI) for Yorkshire should be examined. The IGI can be consulted at LDS Family History Centres, the SOG, IHGS and some County Record Offices and large libraries. This might reveal the marriage of WILLIAM JESSON and MARY HUSTWICK between 1820 and 1831. It might also provide dates of baptism for other children in different parishes of the county.

4. Only a limited search has been carried out in the parish registers of Coston in Leicestershire. The examination of the registers should be extended. This will provide a full listing of references to people with the surname JESSON living in the parish and using the parish church at the end of the 18th century and in the early 19th century. A family tree of the relatives of WILLIAM JESSON senior could be constructed. A marriage of JOHN and ANN JESSON is a prime objective together with a baptism of JOHN between 1760 and 1785. Burials for JOHN and ANN and perhaps the parents of JOHN should be sought.

5. Whether or not a burial for JOHN JESSON and his parents are located in the parish registers, a search could be made in the available probate indexes or calendars to the ecclesiastical courts that had jurisdiction over Coston and the surrounding area. In this way relevant wills or administrations could be located. The appropriate courts would be the Archdeaconry Court of Leicester, the Consistory Court of Lincoln and the Prerogative Court of Canterbury (refer to the Gibson Guide *Probate Jurisdictions: Where to Look for Wills*).

J. ADAMS

Adams of Otham, Kent

(All events took place in Otham unless stated otherwise.)

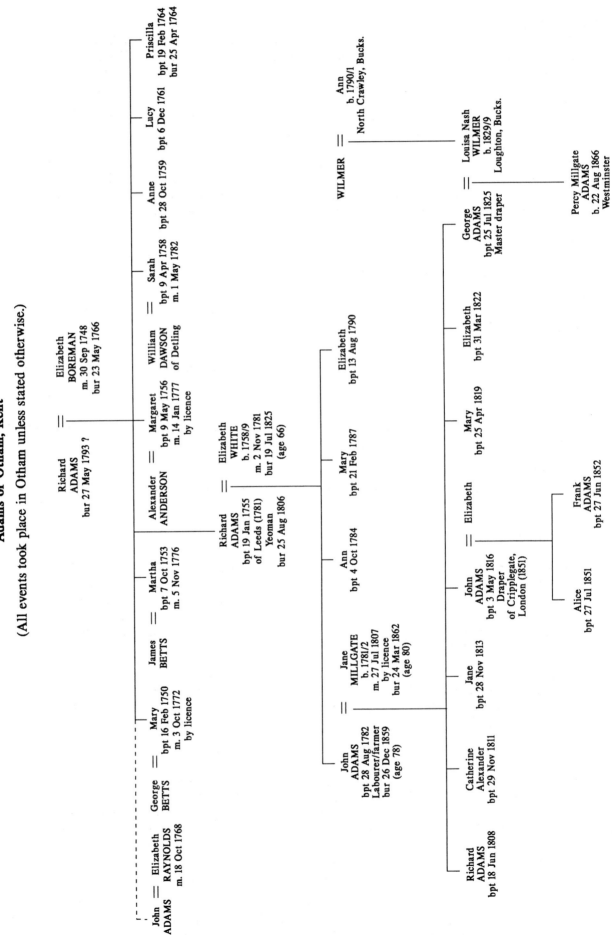

J. ADAMS (continued)

RICHARD senior
Married ELIZABETH BOREMAN on 30th September 1748 in Otham parish church. It is possible that he was buried in the parish in 1793. His wife ELIZABETH had been buried in 1766. Their children were christened in the parish between 1750 and 1764.

RICHARD junior
Married ELIZABETH WHITE in 1781. At that date he was living in the parish of Leeds in Kent. RICHARD appears to have been buried in Otham in 1806 when he was stated to be a 'yeoman from Leeds'. His wife was buried in 1825 aged 66 suggesting a year of birth of 1758/9.

Other children of RICHARD ADAMS senior were baptised and married in the parish church of Otham. It is possible that two of the daughters, MARY and MARTHA married two brothers, GEORGE and JAMES BETTS. The JOHN ADAMS who married in 1768 may have been the oldest son of RICHARD ADAMS senior and have been christened elsewhere shortly after the marriage in 1748.

JOHN senior
Baptised in Otham in 1782, married JANE MILLGATE in 1807. The ages given for JOHN and JANE at their burials suggest that both were born c. 1782.

JOHN junior
Was a draper, like his brother GEORGE, and moved to Cripplegate in London by 1851. However it seems that he returned to the parish to have his two children baptised there.

GEORGE
Was also a draper who had migrated to Westminster by 1866 when his son was born. The middle name given to the child, PERCY MILLGATE ADAMS, was the maiden name of his grandmother.

LOUISA NASH WILMER
Her approximate year of birth can be calculated from the information given to the census enumerator. She had been born in Loughton, Buckinghamshire.

ANN WILMER
Listed as an eighty year old widow, was living with the family in 1871. She too had been born in Buckinghamshire.

To confirm and extend the pedigree:

1. For those marriages of the ADAMS family of Otham which took place by licence, it would be sensible to locate and examine the associated marriage bonds and allegations. These should be found, if they survive, in the appropriate Diocesan Record Office. The identity of this office can be determined by consulting the Gibson Guide *Bishop's Transcripts and Marriage Licences: A Guide to their Location and Indexes*. These documents will provide the approximate ages of bride and groom. In the case of the marriage of a minor, such as MARGARET ADAMS in 1777, the name of the father will probably be recorded.

2. As RICHARD ADAMS junior is stated on two occasions to be of Leeds, a nearby parish, it would be appropriate to examine the parish registers or bishop's transcripts for that locality. These might contain a baptism of JOHN ADAMS circa 1748/9 and confirm if he was the oldest son of RICHARD ADAMS and ELIZABETH (BOREMAN).

3. The ADAMS family were yeoman farmers in Leeds and Otham. They certainly would be expected to have sufficient property and possessions to bequeath these formally in testamentary documents. Such wills or administrations would be dealt with by the probate authorities. The ecclesiastical courts involved would be identified by consulting *The Phillimore Atlas and Index of Parish Registers* or the Gibson Guide *Probate Jurisdictions: Where to Look for Wills*. At a local level these probate documents will be in the Kent County Record Office in Maidstone where the appropriate indexes can be viewed. Any probate documents for testators called ADAMS who lived in this area should be examined. Especially of interest would be documents for either RICHARD ADAMS who died in 1793 and in 1806. There may also be wills for the father and grandfather of RICHARD ADAMS senior.

4. It would also be necessary to locate the baptism of RICHARD ADAMS senior. He would probably have been born between 1710 and 1735. The bishop's transcripts of Otham have only been searched back to 1745/6. The search in these records should be extended to the beginning of the 18th century. If a christening of RICHARD ADAMS is found it would be necessary to search the burial records to ensure that this child did not die as an infant.

J. ADAMS (continued)

5. If the baptism of RICHARD ADAMS is not located in the records of Otham or Leeds, the best way of finding other parishes of interest would be to consult the various Kent marriage indexes. A number of these have been compiled by different individuals for different periods. The relevant names and addresses can be discovered from the Gibson Guide *Marriage, Census and Other Indexes for Family Historians*. If a marriage is found for a RICHARD or JOHN ADAMS between 1700 and 1730, the parish register or bishop's transcripts of these places should be searched.

BIBLIOGRAPHY

District Register Offices in England and Wales
   published by East Yorkshire Family History Society, 7th edition, 1990.

Alumni Cantabrigienses, Part 1 (1250)–1751, 4 volumes; Part 2, 1751–1900, 6 volumes, J. Venn and J.A. Venn.
   published by Cambridge University Press, 1922–1954.

The Survey Gazetteer of the British Isles including Summary of 1931 Census and Reference Atlas, John Bartholomew.
   published by John Bartholomew and Son, 9th edition, 1943.

Crockford's Clerical Directory, 1858.
   published sporadically until 1870, annually thereafter and lately biennially, Church House Publishing for the Church Commissioners for England and the Central Board of Finance of the Church of England.

The Parish and Vital Records List.
   published by Family History Department of The Church of Jesus Christ of Latter Day Saints, 1988.

The Phillimore Atlas and Index of Parish Registers, edited by C. R. Humphery-Smith.
   published by Phillimore and Co., 1984.

Bigland's Gloucestershire Collections, edited by Brian Frith.
   published by Bristol and Gloucestershire Archaeological Society, 1990.

Gibson Guides

All the guides are published by the Federation of Family History Societies.

Bishops' Transcripts and Marriage Licences: A Guide to their Location and Indexes.
   J.S.W.Gibson, 3rd edition, 1988.

Census Returns on Microfilm 1841–1881: A Directory to Local Holdings in Great Britain, Channel Islands, Isle of Man.
   J.S.W.Gibson, 5th edition, 1988.

Coroners' Records in England and Wales.
   J.S.W.Gibson and C. Rogers, 1989.

The Hearth Tax, Other Later Stuart Tax Lists and the Association Oath Rolls.
   J.S.W.Gibson, 1987.

Marriage, Census and Other Indexes for Family Historians.
   J.S.W.Gibson and E. Hampson, 4th edition, 1992.

Probate Jurisdictions: Where to Look for Wills.
   J.S.W.Gibson, 3rd edition, 1986, reprinted 1989.

Record Offices: How to Find Them.
   J.S.W.Gibson and P. Peskett, 5th edition, 1991.

NOTES